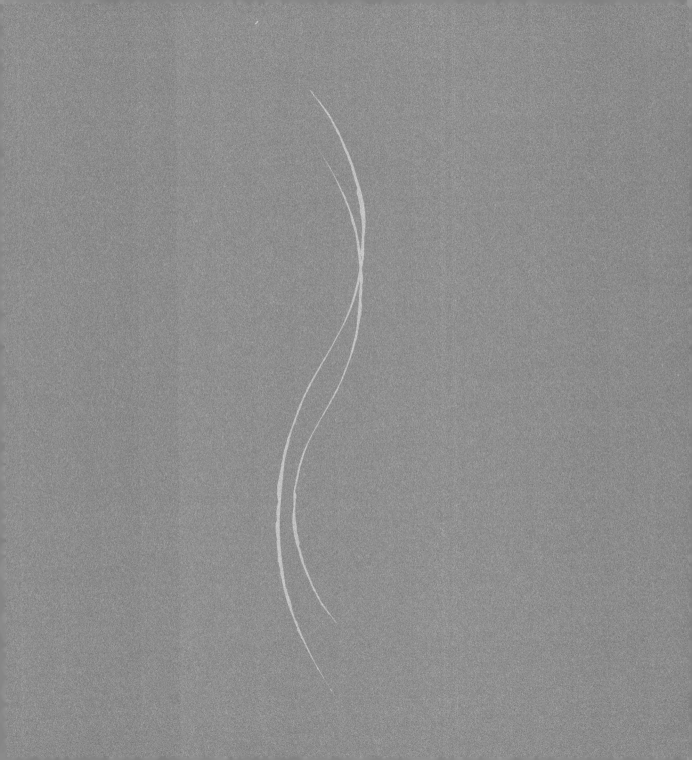

**Books by the same author**

*Surfing as a Dance: How one woman found grace in and out of the water*
*The dharma of surfing: wisdom from the water for life*
*Expanding Green Strategies: Creating change through negotiation*

**Sally MacKinnon Consulting**
www.aliceionamackinnon.com

**Photo credits:**
Tavis Hebler – front and back cover, pages 8, 120, 137, 138, 168
Hannah Jessup – p62, 102, 104, 107, 108, 111, 114, 117, 119, 142, 145, 153, 179
Cal MacKinnon – p18, 22, 39, 54, 70, 88, 91, 92, 150
Alison Gowland - p128, 131, 132, 134
Jennifer Jefferies – p10, 58, 160
Carlos Merlo – p125
Alice MacKinnon – personal collection.

This is a work of creative non-fiction. The events are portrayed to the best of Alice MacKinnon's memory. While all the stories in this book are true, some names and identifying details have been changed to protect the privacy of the people involved.

First published 2023
ISBN: 978-0-646-88045-7

**Design:** Ingrid Schroder, Be Visual Co Pty Ltd / bevisualco.com.au @be.visual
**Printing:** Ingram Spark; Lightning Source

# Becoming a Stillness Ninja

## Reflections on Resilience, Recovery and Love

Alice MacKinnon

I dedicate this book of stories and poems with everlasting love to my wife Jen,
son Huon, brother Cal, granddaughter Ellie and nephews Clancy and Mackie.
Love runs strong in our veins.

*These stories and this book were written and designed in the lands of the Yugambeh and Bundjalung People.*

*This land, its waters and all life have been tended, sung, celebrated, managed and loved for some sixty thousand years by these First Nations People.*

*I acknowledge this land has never been ceded and I pay deep respect to these Traditional Custodians of country and Elders, past, present and emerging of this region and across this continent.*

# Contents

# LOVE ~ 84

# WATER ~ 120

# SPIRIT ~ 148

## CONCLUSION

"
*Quiet as a feather.*
*I hardly move though really*
*I'm traveling a terrific distance.*
*Stillness.*
*One of the doors into the temple.*

"

Mary Oliver

# The power of stillness

I invite you to take a long, slow, deep breath
in through your nose and down into your belly...

Can you feel your belly expand? Pause for a few heartbeats. Now slowly let the breath flow out of your nose or mouth and feel your whole body soften. Then pause for a few heartbeats. Let's do that again. Inhale long, deep and slow, in through the nose and feel your belly expand. Pause. Exhale slowly and feel your body soften. Pause for a few heartbeats.

Can you feel your heart beat? Can you feel the breath moving through your body like the tide?

How do you feel as you breathe in and pause, then breathe out and pause? What are you noticing in your body and your mind? Is there stillness and steadiness? Quietness? Impatience or frustration? I invite you to notice without judgement.

Feel free to keep breathing like this for as long as you like. Perhaps this is the only time in your day that you have stopped, noticed your breath and how your body and mind are feeling. Perhaps this is the only time today you've been still. How does it feel to be still?

Stillness seems to be in short supply these days. Our lives overflow with so much busyness and perpetual motion that our constant companions are often irritation, distraction, impatience and perhaps even a sense of entitlement: 'My responsibilities and commitments are more urgent than anyone else's... I can't stand here in this queue when I have somewhere more important to be...I must go first and fast-track through this situation...'

Does this seem a little familiar?

Yet if we regularly stop, breathe deeply and be still, we can regain perspective of our life. We can reclaim patience, steadiness and even kindness when we practice being still every day. We can also remember we have all the time we need.

I have developed a whole new skillset and mindset. I now believe beyond a shadow of a doubt, that I am loveable and capable of growing exponentially to embrace love, relationship and intimacy skills, vital and healthy longevity, even financial literacy and business success.

I practice stillness like a ninja to harness my mind and cultivate inner peace so I can skilfully ride the waves of life with alignment and grace.

That's what this book is about. Becoming the person I always had the potential to be – warm, kind, joyful, wholehearted, loving, nimble, healthy, unfashionably wholesome, successful and true to myself.

In the spring of 2019, the ground beneath my feet disintegrated. As I scrambled to regain a foothold on my life, it shifted again and again, leaving me reeling and feeling disoriented. It began with a bushfire. It ended three years later when I lost my mountain home and family property.

I applied myself to transformation out of collapse like a martial artist. Each day, over many years, I felt myself becoming more and more skilful at working with inner and outer energies in order to both serve others and flourish.

In amongst those years of groundlessness, free-falling and endings, I chose to begin again. As I write to you dear reader, just before this book of reflections upon resilience, recovery and love goes to print, I realise not only have I begun again, I have become someone entirely new. I have a new name, a new wife, a new home, and a new community.

I practiced stillness daily through sitting meditation. I still do and will continue to, for the rest of my life.

This book of stories, poems and photographs from those critical years is divided into five sections to help bring the light and shadows of this time into perspective. They are not in chronological order – my hope is that in their individuality, they offer you many perspectives of resilience, recovery and love that might help illuminate how to choose life no matter how hard the circumstances.

Fire: dives deep into the 2019 Beechmont bushfire disaster, global climate crisis and the effects of the fire on me, my brother Cal and my mother Joss. It also reveals some of the pathways towards healing that I crafted in order to walk out of that traumatic experience.

Family: offers portraits and snapshots from my early childhood through to my life as a grandmother, revealing patterns of loss and love and how I now choose to move through the world.

Love: is more than the intimate, personal romance I found and actively cultivate with my wife Jen, although there is a good dose of that in here. Our story is mixed in with stories about home and the landscapes of Southeast Queensland and Northern New South Wales that run through my bones.

Water: is my inspiration and solace. These stories connect with the uplift of water and its healing properties...there are stories and poems here that celebrate the relationship I cherish with the ocean, beaches and rivers of Southeast Queensland and Northern New South Wales and in particular with the community of women in this region who are taking up surfing in droves as they grow older.

Spirit: is not a word we use much in public, maybe because it's so easily misinterpreted. Yet here it is in this book about resilience, recovery and love, offered in the form of a few gentle dharma-style reflections about some of the practices and traditions that hold me kindly and were foundational to my healing journey.

Calamity, it turned out, was a gritty gift – deeply disguised for a while, as ruin.

It is my intention and great hope that these stories and poems reach out and help give your own life a feeling of substance, meaning, purpose and coherence. And when our paths cross, as I hope they will, may our hands meet in friendship, trust and solidarity. ◎

> *The effort of the imagination is*
> *to turn the boundary into a horizon.*
> *The boundary says, 'Here and no further.'*
> *The horizon says, 'Welcome'.*

Barry Lopez

# Fire

# The beginning is the end

For over 30 years I lived in a small mountain community
in Southeast Queensland, Australia.

That community is nestled within the McPherson Overlap, a landscape of extraordinary ecological significance and diversity. It's where the northern-most reaches of Australia's temperate forests connect with the southern-most stretch of this country's tropical rainforests. They meet in an explosion of biodiversity in World Heritage-listed Lamington National Park or Woonoongoora which is part of the Gondwana Rainforests of Australia World Heritage Area. This is the most extensive, sub-tropical rainforest under protection, remaining on the planet today.

It is also the home of the Wangerriburra People – the First Nations People of the mountains of Beechmont and Tamborine Mountain as well as the valley of Canungra that separates the two plateaus. This landscape is embedded in the Yugambeh Language Region which is home to eight family or clan groups who are custodians and Traditional Owners of the diverse landscapes between the Logan River at Beenleigh, south of Brisbane; the Tweed River at Tweed Heads, a hair's breadth across the New South Wales border; and the farmlands of Beaudesert and Boonah which are west of the Gold Coast.

I lived in the community of Beechmont, in a sweet 100-year old weatherboard cottage that I called the 'Storybook Cottage' because of its quaint array of silky oak casement windows, external hardwood weatherboards and open fireplace. It was located on the sunrise side of our family property known as The Summit which was right at the top of a mountain at the end of a one-road-in, one-road-out situation. I shared that magnificent two-acre property with my brother Cal, his new partner (then wife) Ash and my mother Joss.

To the west, our property teetered on the edge of Lamington National Park, separated only by privately-owned forest and an uprising of basalt cliffs. This was where Cal's home was located – a 1980s brick and timber building which adjoined Mum's granny flat – a comfortable, spacious, converted double garage.

To the south, we looked up to Mount Roberts, Binna Burra Lodge and a corner of the sky where summertime thunderheads glowered in mountainous storms before they descended upon us in pounding rain and hail.

To the east, across the ridges of Springbrook Plateau, we could glimpse the glimmer of the Coral Sea where it gathered in ruffles and iconic swells around Jellurgal – Burleigh Headland – on the Gold Coast.

Most days dawned with streaming sunlight riding on waves of birdsong across the sky.

For over 20 years I lived in that quirky cottage where all the floors tilted slightly and a raft of dodgy Do It Yourself (DIY) renovations had been tacked onto the original settler farmhouse through the decades. The house was once at the heart of a dairy farm that eventually became the Summit and Timbarra housing developments in the 1970s and 80s. Over the years, these developments grew into close-knit neighbourhoods of about 100 households in total.

It was there I raised my son Huon. He ran with the tribe of three boys who lived next door, most days experiencing a riot of outdoor play after school until the sun sank low and it was time to come home for dinner. He divided his time between the 'Storybook Cottage' and his dad's home ten minutes up the road which was another property of expansive sky and after-school roaming. I saw Huon into the world from that safe haven home when he was 17 years old and he moved to Brisbane to study at university.

When Hu left, I hand-sanded and hand-painted almost every weatherboard, wall and ceiling of that cottage, and restored every silky oak window frame and glass pane. I pulled up dreadful, ancient carpets and brought timber floorboards back to life. I transformed that funky old cottage into my dream home surrounded by flower gardens and plots of herbs. On the kitchen side of the cottage grew a magnificent 90-year old camellia bush that stood almost as high as the roof gutters. Its beautiful pink flowers were layered with so many petals that they reminded

me of lotus blossoms and I'd gently pick five flowers each week to float in water in a cut-glass trifle bowl that used to belong to my grandmother.

Between my home and Cal's stood a heritage-listed macadamia tree we called the Mother Tree, which in turn neighboured a big red cedar. Each winter the red cedar would shed its leaves to reach bare fingers into cold skies. Through July and August every year, I'd watch breathlessly for the first red rosettes of new foliage to appear, signalling the return of spring and warmth to the mountain.

Hanging on chain links from one of the strongest of the red cedar's branches was a long, large timber swing seat and when I was teaching myself the difficult cross-stepping dance of longboard surfing, I practiced constantly on that swing. An hour away from the beach, wrapped up to the eyeballs in woollen winter scarves, is where I learned the art of longboarding in my late forties as I balanced and stepped up and back along the centre panel of that swing, while it shunted forwards and backwards below the cedar's branches and ever-changing foliage.

For over three decades I embedded myself into the Beechmont community – enough time to be considered a local. I loved that place and the people who lived there with all my heart and soul. I wrote love letters, poems and stories to that mountain, sky and forest. I imagined I would never, ever leave. Why would I? I felt entirely nourished by those landscapes and that wonderfully diverse community.

*I loved that place and the people who lived there with all my heart and soul. I wrote love letters, poems and stories to that mountain, sky and forest. I imagined I would never, ever leave.*

But things change. Now I live in the bustling city of the Gold Coast on its southern end, near some of the best surf beaches in the world. I live in a modern suburban home that is filled with light and rainbows. I live with my wife Jen who I love and adore. Harlee the cat and Sherlock the dog (who looks like a hobo but behaves like a gentleman) co-habit with us.

During the transition from mountain to suburbs I changed my name from Sally to Alice.

Instead of an hour's pre-dawn drive, down winding mountain roads to the beach to surf most mornings, it now takes me ten minutes to hit the sand. The serpentine, mangrove-lined Tallebudgera Creek is 700 metres down the road from home – walking

distance to trolley my stand-up paddle board to the public jetty and plop it into the water. It's a tidal haven where I can paddle in peace when I need a break from the hurly burly of the Gold Coast's beaches and traffic.

How did I come to live in a Gold Coast suburb when come-hell-or-high-water, I was living my life to its very end in my quirky storybook cottage on our family property on top of a mountain on the edge of internationally-revered rainforest?

Hell came on Friday 6 September 2019 in a maelstrom of wildfire that devoured our beloved sub-tropical rainforest, the Summit and Timbarra neighbourhoods, Binna Burra Lodge, Cal's home and my surefootedness in the world. It was the worst recorded bushfire in our region and it came at us at the very start of spring after a crazy-dry and windy winter. It was generated by a perfect storm of weather conditions, prolonged drought, zero humidity, excessive fuel load, and high and variable wind.

Our community's history and experience of bushfire in this part of Southeast Queensland could not prepare us for that inferno. Our ancient forest was adapted to rain and our modest homes were not built to withstand such intensity.

In a Guardian article called "*I never thought I'd see the Australian rainforest burning. What will it take for us to wake up to the climate crisis?*" leading international climate scientist Joelle Gergis, who also has a long-standing connection with Lamington National Park and Binna Burra Lodge, said this fire was the result of climate collapse. The article was published just days after the Beechmont fire and referred extensively to it.

The Queensland Rural Fire Brigade said the fire spotted ahead of itself by six kilometres at times and the fire front was some ten kilometres long, a phenomenon they had never encountered before. Incredibly the local Beechmont Rural Fire Brigade had the foresight to fully evacuate our neighbourhoods and Binna Burra Lodge by 5pm on that fateful Friday and no human lives were lost. Eleven homes, most in the Timbarra neighbourhood were destroyed. Cal's home was the only one to be lost in The Summit neighbourhood – from an ember attack that lodged in his uppermost western window. Mum's granny flat was unharmed but uninhabitable while Cal's home was assessed and rebuilt for 11 months, behind high cyclone wire fencing.

Hot on the heels of Beechmont's disaster, I realised I was experiencing Post-traumatic stress disorder (PTSD) from the fire and evacuation, which had in turn triggered unexamined trauma from my early childhood. I quickly began to seek help. At the same time, a series of fiery personal dominoes tumbled, taking down almost every facet of my family life. I experienced three years of mind-bending calamity which culminated at the end of 2021 with the complete loss of my mountain home, the home Cal had rebuilt after the fire, and the 'family' in our family property.

During those roller-coast years – and I must say, roller-coasters have never been my thing – I found love. Twice. The second time it was lasting. My family is healthy. Flourishing even. We all navigated COVID lockdowns successfully during 2020 and 2021. We watched the east coast of Australia burn during late 2019 and 2020 in the worst recorded bushfire season this continent has endured. Then we watched it flood in 2022, in this country's worst recorded rainy season. Whole towns were incinerated or washed away during these years.

Many of us now know what it feels like to lose homes, jobs, security, loved ones, community, peace of mind and perhaps even hope. Many of us also now know how to surface, start again and rebuild everything from the ground up.

I am one of the 'us'. ◎

# Bless the moments

*Bless the moments*
*that bring us undone.*
*The ones that unstitch our hearts*
*and tenderly run their fingers across each string*
*in a lilt like a harp with notes so pure*
*they dance diamonds across the sea.*

*Bless the moments*
*that make us weep.*
*The unexpected, the unhoped-for ones*
*like waking into a breathless morning*
*with not a whisper of wind*
*and the ocean such a shimmering mirror that*
*as we paddle our surfboards east*
*we are redeemed.*

*Bless the moments*
*that still us into silence.*
*The ones so shocking that*
*the critic, the cynic, the tough lover has no comeback*
*and, lost, at last,*
*they sink like stones*
*in water so clear*
*we can see them settle in a huff of sand*
*and come to rest.*

*Bless the moments*
*that whisper us awake.*
*That light, laughter, smile, touch,*
*feather, petal, leaf, tree*
*that windblown nest we rescue from the roadway*
*and cup in our hands as we*
*search for small eggs and*
*tiny signs of life.*
*That kindness we give*
*those gifts we receive.*
*The strength of our ancestors that holds us close*
*and though we walk our paths without their presence*
*we know we carry their lives inside*
*as we finally find our way home.*

> *The system will collapse, if we refuse to buy what they are selling — their ideas, their version of history, their wars, their weapons, their notions of inevitability. Remember this: We be many and they be few. They need us more than we need them. Another world is not only possible, she is on her way. On a quiet day, I can hear her breathing.*

Arundhati Roy

# Under fire

My brother Cal texted me just two words
at 3.30pm on Friday 6 September 2019:
"Leaving now".

Attached to his message was an eerie photo
of a sun on fire, a sky streaming with
smoke, and our favourite backyard forest
trees cast in silhouette.

As I stepped beyond the car park at the Tugun Fruit Market on the southern Gold Coast to check the sky over Beechmont and Binna Burra, Cal rang at the very moment I saw a massive wave of black smoke engulf our mountain.

He said, "The Beechmont firies are running down our driveway. They're crying and telling us we have to leave now. We've got the cats and Mum's passport. We're going now."

Cal and his then-partner Ash took the only road out and made for the coast. That Friday, all the residents of Beechmont's Timbarra and Summit neighbourhoods were evacuated from their homes before nightfall. A bushfire that had started burning a few days earlier near Canungra to the west, had gotten away from the volunteer firefighters. The wind was blowing the embers up to six kilometres ahead of the fire itself and it was bearing inevitably down upon our community.

Our ridge, perched just above World Heritage-listed Lamington National Park, was in the frontline of an inferno raging through the once-moist and mossy valley up the western flank of the mountain.

After a long, dry winter, the last of the moisture in our landscape and air seemed to be sucked dry and now even the rainforest was a tinderbox.

Over 100 adults, children and families left our homes that day, knowing we may never see them again.

Sleep was impossible that Friday night.

In the early hours of Saturday 7 September, the fire that had been crawling around the cliffs below our neighbourhoods was whipped into a frenzy by 60-70 kilometre westerly winds, and an ember storm rained down upon our homes. Despite desperate efforts by an army of firies, almost 20 percent of homes in the Timbarra neighbourhood were destroyed – that's ten out of about 60.

Cal and Ash's home which also had our mother's granny flat attached to it, copped an ember attack through western windows and a wall flashing. While the house still mostly stood, everything inside was incinerated or ruined beyond repair. Cal and Ash lost everything.

Theirs was the only home to be destroyed in The Summit neighbourhood. Somehow my little weatherboard cottage with its tilting timber floors and silky oak casement windows that didn't seal properly, survived completely intact. Mum's granny flat too.

Within 24 hours, Binna Burra Lodge – one of Australia's first nature-based lodges, established in 1933 – had burned to the ground.

When residents were finally and officially allowed home by the police and other emergency services after five days of displacement, the air was still stuffed with smoke and barely breathable. Sirens punctuated our little country road with emergencies, and choppers filled our skies. All I could see left of Binna Burra Lodge from my place was a single column of smoke exhaling into sky.

Beechmont is a little community up in the mountains west of the Gold Coast. It is Wangerriburra land – home to the mountain people and part of the Yugambeh Language Region. This land has been tended and sung for over 60,000 years by a culture that arose from this land and this rainforest.

Lamington was World Heritage-listed for its ecological values in 1994. Its moss-drenched forests are packed with the oldest elements of the world's ferns and primitive plant families dating back to the Jurassic era 200 million years ago. It existed in the age of dinosaurs.

The Binna Burra-Beechmont community where I lived for over 30 years, is filled with ecologists, Landcarers, bush regenerators, farmers, bird watchers, nature guides, writers, poets, artists, musicians,

Courier Mail MARCH 7-8, 2020

QWEEKEND

AFTER THE FIRE

Six months after the Binna Burra blaze, the trauma endures

LEISA SCOTT

local business operators, ambulance officers, fire fighters, tradespeople, teachers, parents, grandparents, teenagers and children.

This community is awake and engaged.

Between 2004 and 2008 as the co-founder and Executive Officer of The Ethos Foundation, a not-for-profit adult sustainability learning centre, I helped organise and host a series of five-day 'Courageous Conversations' at Binna Burra Lodge – about climate change, renewable energy, sustainability, social change and other important issues – with government, business and community leaders.

At the same time, Ethos organised local community campaigns to reduce household energy and water use across Beechmont. This led to a bulk-buy of household solar energy systems across our community.

When coal mining and coal seam gas corporations tried to activate leases in our region – the Scenic Rim Region – Beechmont was one of the first communities to get organised. We worked closely with the good folk of Mount Barney, Mount Tamborine, Beaudesert and beyond to organise public education and media campaigns, community protests, government lobbying and civil disobedience. Eventually we ran those bastards out of the region and the Scenic Rim is now protected under State Government legislation.

The Beechmont community is resilient and quiet and guards its peace and landscapes carefully.

After the bushfire disaster our community was swamped by deep grief. We were shocked to the core and traumatised by this fire and the others that followed it over the next three months. This was the type of fire that southern states of Australia know well in summer but it was an unprecedented, catastrophic firestorm in Southeast Queensland rainforest in the first week of spring.

We lost our homes.

Our rainforest burned.

Our neighbourhood forest animals were injured and killed.

For months after our homes were lost and our community overrun by the main wildfire, we lived in a warzone of smoke, ongoing fires, destruction, burning forest, falling trees, sirens, choppers and water bombing.

We will be forever grateful to the firies – Beechmont's own crews, crews from other country communities and the metropolitan crews.

We were hugely grateful for the incredible on-ground response to our disaster. Government, non-government and community groups were wonderful.

We were overwhelmed by community care, kindness, generosity and love – expressed through home-cooked meals, gifts of money, furniture, hugs and so much more.

We also knew that the best scientific, fire and ecology specialists had applied themselves to sound forest management practices for many, many years; while successive federal and state governments had ripped budgets to shreds in key organisations like the CSIRO and National Parks. We knew that federal and state government legislation that protected our forests, wild rivers and human communities had been decimated by climate-denying governments at all levels for years.

Dear readers, I want you to hear, understand and help tell this story.

Please use it and use Beechmont and Binna Burra to help create decisive change. No more climate denying. No more corporate and political lies. No more polluting. No more moving the deck chairs on the Titanic.

We must rise together. Not just for humans but for the whole community of life. With peace. Without violence. With compassion. With solidarity.

Why does the Binna Burra-Beechmont bushfire experience matter?

In a country where bushfire is common, why worry about my community's misfortune?

Binna Burra is rainforest. Subtropical rainforest. It seldom burns. A wildfire of this catastrophic scale in World Heritage-listed rainforest was unheard of until 2019.

*We must rise together.
Not just for humans but for the
whole community of life.*

Binna Burra and Beechmont are living examples of what happens when our climate collapses. When regional temperatures rise; when seasons fail; when rainfall disappears and a rainforest becomes an inferno in an extreme weather event.

Do not let politicians tell you otherwise.

Do not let polluting corporations seduce or distract you with shiny stuff.

Do not let anyone bully you into thinking that the Beechmont wildfire was normal in any way.

Binna Burra-Beechmont in September 2019 was a living example of the global climate emergency.

Do not forget my community.

Use us as a vivid, living tool to help tell the story of climate emergency and create decisive change. ◎

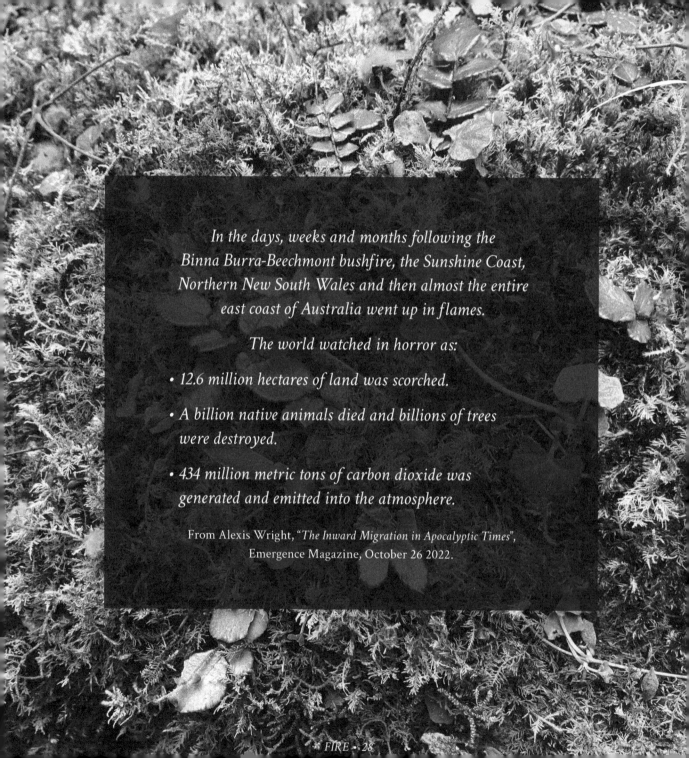

*In the days, weeks and months following the*
*Binna Burra-Beechmont bushfire, the Sunshine Coast,*
*Northern New South Wales and then almost the entire*
*east coast of Australia went up in flames.*

*The world watched in horror as:*

• *12.6 million hectares of land was scorched.*

• *A billion native animals died and billions of trees*
*were destroyed.*

• *434 million metric tons of carbon dioxide was*
*generated and emitted into the atmosphere.*

From Alexis Wright, "*The Inward Migration in Apocalyptic Times*",
Emergence Magazine, October 26 2022.

# Faith

A poet once named the act of writing poetry
in mythical terms.
It was, she said, like
seizing a dragon's tail as
the great beast thundered overhead; then,
sprinting, tearing, racing, panting,
galloping in its wake,
to snatch up pen and paper and
frantically spin words into wide-eyed life
before being consumed.

I have clutched that dragon's tail.
I have spun those words from thin air into
astonishing, shimmering nets that
turned their gaze towards eternity.
I have sung the siren's song of earth and sea,
I have spoken for the trees.
I have been consumed.

Six months have passed since
a different beast devoured our rainforest
world with fire;
crushing us, choking our words.
Today I choose to claw my way back
to poetry.
I sense no dragon's tail yet;
but there are grey whispers through the mist on dark
– the wallaby mob is on the move.
And this is the season of biblical dawns;
god-head cumulous
extending its reach to bless the hearts of all life here
now that the rains have come.

As empty-handed as I feel
I watch the world again with poet's eyes and
tenderly place the moon
the dahlias
the sou'westerlies
the jaunty butterflies
like sacraments upon my tongue,
reclaiming my faith in the poet's life.

Three black cockatoos slide across the sky.
I find a feather in the grass.

# Four weeks to the day

It's a beautiful morning. Soft. Calm. The hobo dog is asleep at the end of my bed.
It's exactly four weeks to the day that our big-sky mountain-world was turned on its head,
tilted and toppled from its axis, and everything was forever changed.

Exactly four weeks ago the air was charged with smoke. Out by the bird bath, as I filled it for the neighbourhood animals that had been drinking there more and more often as the moisture in the atmosphere disappeared during the last week of winter, a single flake of black ash drifted lazily from the sky.

I caught it between two fingers and, deep in thought, rubbed it into a dark smudge.

Then I climbed the long ladder onto the roof of my cottage and crawled around on my knees until they bled, cleaning leaves and twigs out of every gutter. Something felt terribly wrong.

By dusk that Friday, every single resident of The Summit and Timbarra neighbourhoods at Beechmont had left. Evacuated, often with teary hugs, by our local firies.

I heard later how eerie it felt for the firies during their patrols through our empty streets, keeping watch over our empty homes. Bless them a million times over.

Binna Burra Lodge, the old heritage-listed guest house, was emptied of guests and staff too.

Our mountain stood poised upon its own cliff edge. Waiting.

Overnight it came.

A ten kilometre-long, two kilometre-wide wildfire spotting ahead of itself by six kilometres (our firies later told us there has never been such a huge bushfire with such a long length of ember spotting, ever recorded in Queensland).

Through the unique, world-renowned, world-revered subtropical rainforest of Lamington National Park – home of Jurassic era plants and rare, vulnerable and endangered species of life – it roared.

> Ring the bells that still can ring;
> forget your perfect offering;
> there is a crack, a crack in everything;
> that's how the light gets in.

Leonard Cohen

As our local National Park ranger said afterwards, it came so hard and fast it left a cascade of death in its wake...so many animals gone, too slow to escape. So many plants and ferns and mosses and trees gone when that beast roared through this protected and passionately-loved place.

The fire was so hot that the leaves on the trees didn't burn, they 'froze' in the direction the inferno-wind was howling.

When it hit our ridge, the cliffs below our neighbourhoods held it back for a while and it crawled malevolently around the base of those blessed rocks, biding its time.

In my family's first sleepless night of displacement, scattered between Palm Beach, Brunswick Heads and Bangalow, we hung onto every morsel of news from our firie friends. We imagined those fingers

of flame seeking purchase across the cliffs while fire trucks and quiet heroes prepared for the onslaught above; like a biblical battle of David and Goliath proportions.

We will never know exactly how desperate the firefighters must have felt when the westerly wind whipped itself up to 60-70 kilometres per hour and hurled a firestorm of embers and flames over our homes.

We do know at one stage the volunteer Rural firefighters retreated because their equipment wasn't built to cope with that level of ferocity. We also know the Urban firefighters stepped in with all their state-of-the-art equipment but even so, they endured at least one burn-over where they were forced into their shuttered trucks to survive.

In the Timbarra neighbourhood ten homes were burned to the ground. A month later one still partly stood as an eerie skeleton, some were piles of tin and twisted metal, and some had been cleared so that all that was left to show of the years, the decades of life and love within them, were split concrete slabs.

Numerous sheds and outhouses burned and roofing iron on nearby homes was 'cooked' and no longer watertight.

On Mount Roberts just up the road, Binna Burra Lodge, the former manager's house and the Groom family home "Alcheringa" turned to ashes.

And my brother's home, mostly intact from the outside, was gutted and everything lost internally from ember attack.

Our neighbourhood lookouts and ridge, where so many of us found silence and solitude on golden afternoons, became scorched earth and an agony of annihilated trees.

My god.

Slowly, very very slowly, we began to ever so tentatively, ever so tenderly, reach out and connect as new and old neighbours and friends.

This catastrophe burned us all up emotionally and we knew we would never be the same again.

Our two small neighbourhoods overlooking Lamington, were brutally thrust into the frontline of climate collapse in a country governed by climate-change-deniers of many persuasions.

We experienced deep shock and deep grief.

It took us weeks to find the wherewithal to even start looking for the methods, the processes, and the practices that might begin to heal us.

We felt raw but we tried things like deep breathing, acupuncture, afternoon tea, counselling, information sharing, shy hugs, bear hugs, house cleaning, video storytelling, social media-ing, painting, research, walking, music, community singing, bits of work and study if our minds allowed it, and of course, there were the practicalities of rainwater tank testing and insurance-driven demolition, rebuilding, and renovation.

We learned about the small and big things that helped us take one breath, one step. One breath, one step.

I burst into tears at Spec-Savers one day when the nice young assistant asked for my address.

I'd spoken my address so many times as a place of household carnage in the weeks after the fire, that this time, sitting in the brightly-lit store in the home of mega-consumption that is Robina Shopping Town, I tipped over the edge. Our family property, our spiritual home felt contaminated with sorrow and grief. Just the hobo dog and I living there in my storybook cottage and it felt desolate.

There I was, four weeks to the day, from that fateful day.

The "deer in the headlights" trauma seemed to have left my body thanks to vigorous deep breathing exercises and acupuncture.

I'd had three decent nights' sleep in a row – a miracle of epic proportions.

I was journaling again and preparing to return to a full load of work running my exercise classes at a Gold Coast community centre.

My family was alive and well.

Mum was content in a cabin in a holiday park by the Brunswick River. She had already been there housesitting for a friend when the fire hit and I'd organised to extend her stay there for many months in advance with some of the house insurance paying her rent.

Cal and Ash had married in small beachside ceremony a few weeks after the fire, staking their claim for happiness in the midst of losing all their worldly possessions and home. They were staying in a comfortable, furnished house ten minutes up the road, again using some of the insurance payout for rent.

Huon and his wife Sammy had also revealed the news of their first pregnancy. How exciting! They were all healthy – glowing in fact and the baby was due in March 2020.

I was, four weeks after the fire, a sister-in-law and a grandmother-in-waiting.

In amongst this slow, tender recovery – like the tiniest bright green grasslings appearing out of the scorched soil – I felt myself returning to life; a new life that held the deepest sorrow and the deepest soulfulness at its core, alongside the potential return of joy.

*It's a beautiful morning. Soft. Calm. The hobo dog is asleep at the end of the bed. It's exactly four weeks to the day that our big-sky mountain-world was turned on its head, tilted and toppled from its axis, and everything was forever changed.* ◎

# My story

I am of forest.
I am of tree consumed by fire
now regenerating
now running the ridges of the Coomera River;
a eucalypt of the McPherson Overlap.

After we burned
I gave myself to Hades and travelled
the deepening routes of mycorrhizal,
uncultivating myself
in a journey of remembering desolation,
despair and
the sacred sorrow of deep time,
where lifeless leaves rattle like pages
in abandoned libraries
and books that burned to the ground
lie sobbing in ashes at our feet.

Human knowledge of this time is so naïve.
We are blind to both the nuances and the thundering
southerlies that
roar across Mount Roberts,
now unsheltered from the world.

But with the return of the rain come the birdwing
butterflies, congregating on poetic greens and blossoms.
Rainforest moths throw themselves at the bathroom
light in a snowstorm of powdery wings
signalling through the night that there is still life.

I am wedded to this place so keenly now that it moves
through me like the tide.
I teeter on the precipice of mythic expression and
take my leave from tidy daylight speech to plunge my
hands into the underworld of soulful roots and fungi.
As I speak for this soil,
we shiver like Wild Things in the wind
in communion
in recognition
and darkness holds me like a lover.

Like a mono-chromatic handmade photograph hung
in the sky to dry
the full moon sets in the west
tangled in a web of scudding clouds.
White cockatoos mill raucously at dusk
their wings like blank pages gusting above the canopy.
There is heartbreaking intimacy in the curl of a leaf
resting by the roadside.
There are quiet skies as my story waits to be told.

> **"**
>
> *You are going to feel like hell if you never write
> the stuff that is tugging on the sleeves in your
> heart – your stories, visions, memories, songs:
> your truth, your version of things, in your voice.
> That is really all you have to offer us,
> and it's why you were born.*
>
> **"**
>
> Anne Lamott

# Losing my mind

I wondered how I would ever return to everyday life as
weeks and months stuttered and stalled in the wake of the fire.

It felt like my community, my family and I had lost
our innocence to the arrival of climate crisis in our
midst and there was nothing we could do about it.

I felt heartbroken that all the decades of research,
work and hope – all of that environmental activism,
consulting, education and communication I'd
immersed myself in professionally and as a community volunteer between my 20s and 50s – had fallen
on deaf ears. Now the worst possible climate collapse scenario was coming to pass in my own backyard, in my own lifetime, and in my awake, engaged
community that valued peace, sanctuary, connection and Mother Earth above all else.

I was heartbroken and fucking furious.

I felt a fierceness and white-hot clarity about what
I thought was important. I knew I'd call bullshit for
what it was, especially with people who had agendas
that were self-serving and not for the good of all.

I also felt a brokenness and extreme vulnerability
that came from experiencing a natural disaster that
was entirely beyond human control, let alone indi-
vidual control.

The emergency text warnings during the firestorm
still haunted me: "…leave immediately…" "…too late
to leave, seek shelter…"

We'd never seen warnings like that before in the
Beechmont community. With an inferno upon you
and all roads closed or impassable, where would you
seek shelter? In your burning home? In your car?
In your rainwater tank? We'd had no experience
or history of such life-threatening emergencies.
We were rainforest people.

And there was the feeling of helplessness.
The hauntedness of evacuating our homes knowing
we may never see them again. Some neighbours
never did see their homes again.

hope that all was well enough. As we drew closer though, we saw the smashed and fire-stained front doors swinging agape in the westerly wind.

As Cal stepped across the threshold of the doorway into the charred ruins of his and Ash's home, he slumped, all the life-energy for a moment, free-falling out of him. Everything was gone, burned up in a scene of horror movie proportions.

In hindsight, I also know that's the moment when long lost, unresolved early childhood trauma was triggered in my nervous system. In an instant, the ghost of a small family of three – a young mother and two small children – escaping from a nightmare of chaos and violence, lodged itself inside my consciousness.

After we found Cal's ravaged and desolate home, I could only engage with immediate family. I stuck like emotional glue to my brother and not even the closest of Beechmont friends could entice me out. Cal, Ash and I made a deal to protect Mum from the sight of their home and the devastation of the Timbarra neighbourhood and surrounding forest, by ensuring she spent her time in Brunswick Heads at the cabin she was renting. I took on direct contact and oversight of her so Cal and Ash could focus entirely on rebuilding their home and their lives. The only gear they had at that time, was what they had evacuated with and most of that was related to each of their university studies. They were virtually starting from scratch.

Day-after-day the three of us met on-site with kind-efficient insurance assessors and entered,

I will go to my grave remembering the harrowing walk up Cal's driveway on the Sunday after the fire went through. We'd been to the first emergency community meeting at Canungra and had wangled our way into the police convoy taking residents up to The Summit and Timbarra neighbourhoods to check homes and livestock.

As the police van let us out at the top of our street I registered instantly that my Storybook Cottage was intact. I gripped Cal's hand as we entered his driveway and intently scanned through the trees to see the state of his home. We could barely breathe. Then we saw the house, standing, and we dared to re-entered and re-entered the toxic, frightening, burned out home. We gave our details, made grateful, stilted small talk with the assessors and prayed that our policies would hold strong. They did.

We made forays to community disaster meetings with other haunted neighbours.

In between the long stretches of hell, we laughed in snorts at the black humour of the firestorm's destruction. Cal's undies melted and dripping like a Salvador Dali masterpiece on the indoor drying rack at the top of the stairs.

"Do you think they're dry yet?" he asked. We fell about until our bellies ached.

Most of the time I felt mute, frozen and sleepless.

Sometimes I thought I was losing my mind. I couldn't focus on or remember things. I felt overwhelmed by noise, light, wind, and even the ocean. I didn't know where my mind had gone and I hoped hibernation was the worst-case scenario. As the southern hemisphere swung decisively towards springtime storms and humidity, I prayed my mind would begin to stir, to stretch, to shake its sleepy, shaggy self and blink open its eyes.

My own process of evacuation played itself out often in my mind during long, dark, solitary nights. Anyone who says they're not attached to their worldly goods has never had the experience of sudden evacuation. It's not just dispensable 'stuff'. It's stories of our lives in concert with the people we love and the gifts we've given and received, sometimes across generations and ancestral lines.

I thought about the artwork I'd reluctantly left behind that evacuation day. Our local friend and renowned landscape painter Dave Groom's first ever oil painting of the creeks and ocean of K'gari – Fraser Island. His William Robinson-inspired rainforest triptych that I paid off for months on the occasion of my engagement to Huon's dad David back in 1993.

Cal was once a professional photographer and fine art student and in my home I displayed his photographic portrait of his son Clancy at age 10 – a poignant coming of age image with his grandmother showing him how to manually knot a neck tie.

There was also the brilliant work from his Circus Diary exhibition of two female acrobats preparing for their act, that I loved so much. I'd left it all behind.

There was Huon's beautiful oboe that I'd relentlessly saved for and given to him in his last year of primary school.

My art deco lamp and my grandmother's cut glass bowls and cannisters with silver lids.

A lifetime's collection of preciousness alongside the purely functional – tea pots and cups, saucepans and the soft cushions loved so much by the hobo dog.

The whole freak'n house that I had been sanding, painting and restoring by hand for years.

It wasn't just stuff by any stretch of the imagination. And while I still had all of mine, Cal and Ash and ten other local households had lost all of theirs.

As days and weeks and months passed I looked for my mind again. I looked for it in the deep roots of tall trees. I looked for it in underground caves and caverns. I looked for it in the wreckage of fire-stormed neighbourhoods and in tightly-crammed boxes shoved into the back of dark cupboards. Eventually I sought therapeutic help and my long journey to healing and recovery began. ◎

# Alchemy

*In the long silence before dawn*
*I dip my head into the river of stars to*
*sense the wind.*
*The ocean calls.*
*Today she is like heaven*
*alive with diamond light*
*and we revel in each other's company while*
*the sky tilts towards winter.*

*I have been climbing back up,*
*out of the deep of grief, trauma*
*and nervous system breakdown.*
*Thanks to hard work and help*
*I begin to take my place in the world again*
*showing up to life and love.*
*I know this love is the crucible*
*for this work*
*in the spaces where the chambers of the heart*
*the mind, the body and the brain meet and*
*leaden weight runs with gold.*
*Here now, I become the alchemist of my life.*

*Mother Earth, it is your daughter here.*
*What do you have to tell me?*
*The mother of all mothers says,*
*"Your grief is my gift to you;*
*for in the wounding lies the key*
*to your healing."*
*We breathe together – all life as one,*
*until our last breath surrenders*
*and we yield.*

"
*Like a traveller on a train, we can put down our bags.*
*We can relax our grip and trust in the unfolding of life.*
*Do not worry. There is a web of life into which we are*
*born, from which we can never fall.*
"

Jack Kornfield

# The healing season

I want to talk about healing.

Two years after the fire, my pocket-sized vegie garden in the suburbs was flourishing. In late winter I had made my first harvest and shades of green filled my nostrils – a handful of sweet lettuce leaves, spicy coriander and buttery baby spinach – just enough for a delicious lunch.

I used to live in the mountains but I couldn't continue my life there so I moved to the suburbs of the southern Gold Coast to be near the beach. I rented a tiny studio under a family home for six months before Jen and I met and then moved in together.

My tiny, solitary studio was located on a street where a eucalypt forest ran a spectacular amphitheatre around my new neighbourhood. Each morning the dawn chorus spilled over my sleepy shoulders as I walked the hobo dog and marvelled at this place. There was the novelty of streetlights, footpaths and a corner store. There were close-proximity neighbours, and the sounds of the family living upstairs filtered into my open-plan living space where the bedroom connected to the kitchen and the loungeroom.

I landed there at the end of June 2021, swapping that breathtaking vista of Mount Roberts and Binna Burra (now without its iconic slab timber lodge), for a cocoon-like space that held warmth in winter and opened to cool breezes in summer.

It seemed an appropriate change of habitat for a woman in her late 50s in the final stages of navigating her way out of two years of trauma. A woman in the last of the mush between caterpillar and transformative butterfly.

It took a long time of living as mush to find my feet again, patiently sitting it out while I learned to walk again step-by-step, back into the world after the bushfire.

⌢

I'm sitting in a quiet room on a grey linen couch, tapping my right index and middle finger across my head, forehead, cheekbone, chin and finally

chest. As I tap I look intently across the room to Mon, following her lead and repeating a series of statements she speaks as we tap.

*"Even though I feel teary and tight in my chest as I remember evacuating my home, I trust and believe in myself to start again..."*

Three times we tap and I repeat her statements as she adjusts them slightly each time to call up greater strength and resilience from deep inside me. Then I close my eyes and take two deep breaths, noticing what I'm feeling in my body as I exhale. Feet are grounded. Tingling in my fingers. Tightness at the base of my skull. An easing of tension and tears.

Mon is a trauma therapist who uses Radical Exposure Therapy (RET) to defuse and better store trauma 'landmines' within the body and mind. This means I no longer accidentally trip over them or have them blow up in my face, to destroy relationships, jobs and inner peace. Radical Exposure Therapy works a treat on my nervous system, and both childhood trauma and recent bushfire and other family ruptures have largely been put to bed. After a year of this therapeutic processing I can look those events squarely in the eye and authentically speak of them out loud.

My life feels vastly better by working regularly and consistently with a qualified, warm, experienced and highly skilled therapist like Mon.

Deep breathing is an essential part of the conversation between us. I'm good at deep breathing because steadying, calming breath-based practices (sitting meditation, qigong and yoga), have been central to my life for over a decade.

Modern western science is recognising the immense value of practising forms of stillness and conscious deep breathing every day. These practices meet the nervous system through the vagus nerve which in turn helps to regulate the heart rate, digestion and emotions. Greater physical and emotional space is created to first centre ourselves and then respond, rather than lash out when we feel triggered. These practices allow us to notice our heightened emotions, pause, breathe deeply, look around, then come back to ground and our calm thinking mind. They steady and soothe us when the world seems out of control.

I am a devoted practitioner of Japa breathing (long, slow, deep breathing with a mantra), sitting meditation, yoga and qigong and I have felt their deep benefits over many years. Showing up to these practices each day changed my life from a mania of doing into a steadiness of being through most of my 50s. *And yet, (and this is vitally important), on their own without therapeutic intervention, these practices were not enough to bring me through the years of back-to-back traumatic events. That's why I needed the skilled therapy that Mon gave me.*

~

I'm standing on the sand breathing deeply. Weathered coastal rainforest rises at my back, leaning in to hold me steady. One step at a time, courage muscled up inside, I approach my great love – the ocean – and slide my purple longboard across shining liquid. I stretch my body along its length and begin to paddle towards rolling green waves. Glancing skyward, I laugh out loud as a brahminy kite sweeps across blue, then I cry with happiness, surrendering myself again to joy after the agonising weeks of physical and emotional overwhelm I experienced following the fire.

It takes courage to do this. This surrendering again to beauty, delight and joyfulness after trauma and tragedy. Believing that I deserve to feel happiness again.

~

The journey towards recovery and healing takes time, especially if the initial traumatic event triggers, like a line of tumbling dominoes, a series of subsequent upheavals and unintended consequences in one's life.

For a long time after the fire, I felt mute. The quirky, glorious moments that used to punctuate my days became invisible to me for many months. I despaired. I committed over and again to seeing life fresh and new, and I stumbled and fell as one event after another devoured my optimism and creativity.

Gradually, over blurry days and sleepless nights, I began to heal. Two years on, and no longer living at Beechmont, I felt myself blossoming into a new energy and freshness for life. I was not the same person I was before the fire exploded across our lives. The woman who climbed down the ladder from clearing the gutters of her roof at midday on

Friday 6 September 2019 and then evacuated to the coast an hour later with her most precious, irreplaceable and vital possessions, became another woman altogether.

I learned that terrible things can happen to anyone and that climate collapse is a real and present danger, even in our own backyards. I became cognisant of and eternally grateful for modern medicine and the highly skilled doctors and nurses who save the lives of those most precious to us. I knew even the strongest among us can shatter and break. My heart became so tender that I could sit with the grieving and hold a space of unconditional kindness and love. I learned to bear witness. I calmly set boundaries for my own good. I discovered I could heal, start over and grow pocket-sized gardens in the suburbs. And I remembered how to lift my eyes to the sky and laugh out loud with pure joy and the deepest of thanks for another chance at life. ◎

# Radiance

*Winter radiance is exploding all about me on these dazzling days.*
*The ocean is such a crystalline lake and the horizon so razor-etched*
*that I could almost stretch an arm east and*
*wrap it around the whole wide world,*
*hugging it to my heart forever, so*
*there will be no more tragedy or trauma,*
*no more casualties or collateral damage*
*from God's unfathomably careless ways.*

*On these literally-freezing mornings on the*
*beautiful-one-day-perfect-the-next Gold Coast;*
*(how did it ever get advertised by that name?),*
*I leave the house wearing so many inadequate layers of clothes and rainbow socks,*
*that I look like a refugee from summer,*
*carrying my wardrobe upon my back as I breathe steam into the bowl of blue sky*
*that's dawned after nine months of rain.*

*Healing happens in a myriad of ways in its own sweet and sorrowful time.*
*One day it's agonisingly incremental with steps so small a snail could sail by with a satisfied smile.*
*It's a miracle on others and in a nano-second we are transformed forever,*
*never to be the same again.*
*And some days it happens from the stories pressed inside the hard, white covers of a book*
*from a home in the past tense,*
*with chapters that you thought you'd closed in order to begin anew.*
*A book with stories that like butterflies, brush my cheeks with soft wings saying,*
*here is my heart and mine and mine, broken and bruised too...*
*...here take these hearts and hold them to your own;*
*Let them warm and cradle and soften you,*
*Let them knit you in again to a life that is, more often than not,*
*trustworthy and safe;*
*so you may smile and love radiantly again.*

What would you have to
let go of to be at peace?

"

Jack Kornfield

# Family

# The naming

Apparently, my birth – according to my mother, who by the way,
has never been a reliable witness – was quiet, calm and happy.

As she would have it, my Dad was off playing golf at the time, but as Dad died from a gunshot wound to the head after enduring years of schizophrenia and isn't around for me to check the birth-golf story with, I can only take my mother's version of that.

I was named Sally Anne MacKinnon. MacKinnon with a capital K for my Dad's lineage – the MacKinnons of Skye, the island in Scotland – though there is also some southern United States in our patriarchal blood too.

Sally and Anne were the agreed-upon first and second names. No family history to it and note, Sally is separate to Anne. It's not Sally-Anne in one breath, it's just plain Sally, with Anne as the middle name.

Just plain Sally, a small child who loved dolls, spent her first seven years of life in a family situation mired with mental illness and violence.

Dad – Michael Randolph – it transpired, had severe schizophrenia and suffered from bouts of psychosis. Mum – Jocelyn Helen – was the odd one out in a middle-class family who, if her childhood stories are to be believed, was an adventurer, and an extremely eccentric and creative person.

In my early 50s, Mum told me in a long-awaited, brutally honest conversation, that she had been terrorised most nights by Dad who kept a gun and a hunting knife under the marriage bed. She used to wonder at times what affect her screams were having on little Sally lying in her bed in her bedroom down the hall. That conversation explained why I'd had such trouble getting to sleep and staying asleep my whole life.

When I was seven and my brother Cal, two, Jocelyn Helen found the wherewithal and opportunity to pack us up and leave the violent home in the western suburbs of Sydney to start our lives over as a family of three in Northern New South Wales and then Southeast Queensland.

Her parents, my maternal grandparents Helen and Richard (Nanny and Poppop), were endlessly supportive, kind and generous. They helped buy our new home in Murwillumbah when we first moved north and then again when we moved to Labrador on the Gold Coast. Most school holidays Mum, Cal and I would stay with them in their Bellevue Hill home in Sydney's eastern suburbs. I remember them with enormous love and affection. They were a constant source of warmth and safety.

After we left Dad, he spent time incarcerated in mental institutions, though he also stayed connected with his older brother Sandy and Sandy's family (who elegantly, also stayed connected with us). At the age of 42, Dad took his own life.

From the age of seven I was surrounded with the love and family ties of grandparents, cousins, aunties and uncles, and I think young Sally's life looked and felt quite happy. There were inexplicable jolts every few years, like being sent to boarding school at the age of ten; and then being left behind on the Gold Coast at 17 when Mum took 13-year old Cal down to Geelong, Victoria where she'd found a job as a house matron at a boarding school. But those were the days before children had much say in their lives and so Cal and I took such jolts on the chin and did the best we could living our youthful lives. There was no abuse, neglect or violence, so in many ways we were lucky.

Sally, just plain Sally, who eventually shortened her name to Sal, got on with her life. Education right through to a PhD in 2004. Work and career, which at times became all-absorbing in a way that felt like workaholism. Marriage to David and the birth of our beloved son Huon Mandela, named after the ancient Tasmanian pine tree and the South African hero of democracy, Nelson Mandela.

There was a difficult and damaging divorce and Hu

divided his time between his Dad's and my homes. I worked tirelessly to stay calm and grounded; poured myself into being a loving mother; and contributing to a greener, fairer world through environmental education and community work. Life was frantically busy and I also had a shared family home and property to help maintain and care for.

On my 46th birthday, during a camping holiday with Hu at Lennox Head in Northern New South Wales, I learned to stand up on a surfboard. In a flurry of whitewater dreaming, I felt my spirit ignite after all those years of adapting, fitting in, not making a fuss and working hard.

Surfing connected my mind, body, spirit, heart and brain in the most uplifting and joyful ways and I finally came home to myself and Mother Nature. I learned how to play again and Sal the Surfer was born.

Over the next few years not only did my own surfing evolve, but I also had the undreamed-of opportunity to become a professional surf instructor working predominantly with women. I crafted my own style of instructing based on mindful breathing, yoga, mind-body-ocean alignment and ways to face one's fears head-on.

That opportunity to teach surfing arose during a mid-life career reinvention when I released over 20 years of professional and community environmental education and re-trained in fitness, yoga, surf and qigong instructing.

It was the most wonderful relief to shift my gaze and energy from the frantic reactivity of environmental action to working directly with people around their physical and emotional health. To offer fun, laughter and connection indoors and out. To help bring people home to themselves in the

same way I had come home to myself through surfing. Sal was a very happy and fulfilled woman for many years.

As you know, dear reader, a firestorm broke over my home of Beechmont in the spring of 2019. Everything changed and despite the valiant efforts of so many of us to recover our easy camaraderie and creativity I could no longer cope with life on that mountain.

When people and whole communities experience traumatic events like natural disasters, the axis of our world tilts precariously and no matter what types and levels of therapy one engages with, what's happened can't unhappen and what's been seen and heard, can't be unseen or unheard. A profound vibrational or energetic shift seems to occur and nothing returns to its old ways. Paths to recovery and renewal most certainly open up, but neither recovery nor renewal is the same as return. One must keep walking into the unknown for some time.

Just plain Sally and Sal the Surfer kept walking through two major series of therapy focused on PTSD; the first just months after the fire, the second and much longer series began well over a year later and lasted for a year.

It was in that second round of therapy with the expert help of Mon, the trauma therapist, that 58-year old Sal had the chance to go back in time and see more clearly what little five-year old Sally had experienced.

Mon and I covered an awful lot of ground and some awful personal history. At times it was excruciatingly painful and it took stamina and all my mindfulness practices to keep body and mind intact. I will never ever regret a second of that therapeutic work though. It was life-changing to come to terms with my early childhood, my Dad's mental illness and behaviour; and incredibly, to see much more clearly my Mum's erratic and maddening behaviour patterns and how deeply they had influenced my own. Decades of patterns were laid bare and I learned new ways of communicating and regulating my own emotions and behaviour.

Towards the end of the work with Mon, I drove away from one of our sessions and had the distinct feeling that I had outgrown my first and second

*Alice has always been far and away my favourite name... to me it conjured up sweetness, curiosity, creativity and a capacity to roll with the weirdness of life.*

birth names. Sally. Anne. What a strange feeling but I sat with the awkwardness and let myself dream about a name I might choose if I were to rename myself.

Alice has always been far and away my favourite name. I had always wished Alice was my name instead of Sally. To me it conjured up sweetness, curiosity, creativity and a capacity to roll with the weirdness of life. Think "Alice in Wonderland" if you will, and Alice's wide-eyed ability to journey through the strangest of lands with the strangest of creatures and maintain her composure, equanimity and wits. What a girl.

I wanted to be that woman.

Over the course of weeks I sat with the possibility of naming myself anew and eventually I did. I chose Alice and then a second name to my liking – Iona – after the sacred Scottish island which is also connected to the MacKinnon clan. That's a nod to the mystery and wilds of the Hebridean Isles and the resilient 'saltwater women' who are my ancestors.

When I publicly announced my new names on Facebook (of course!), after speaking privately to my family and closest friends; I was very careful to honour Sally Anne and my parent's naming of me at birth. I didn't want to 'kill off' little or big Sallys because they had seen me through so much of my life including the hardest and happiest of times.

At one point a friend suggested that Sally had navigated the boat that took me across the dangerous rushing river of my life so far, midwifing me to the far shore where Alice could step onto steady ground and guide me into the expansive season of my life. I liked that metaphor very much because it paid deep respect to the strength and resilience of Sally, who continues to live inside me with all her wisdom from experience, while allowing me to evolve into Alice and all her hopes and dreams.

As my naming transition gathered momentum and the inevitable dilemmas of life arose, I found myself asking myself, *"what would Alice do?"* and calling up new and different perspectives and energies. It felt refreshing and liberating. This Alice was quite a woman! She had a lot of schtik, an active bullshit detector, and a capacity to say 'no'. She had a great zest for life too. And she was eminently capable of change, which is a good thing because from the moment I chose her, my life transformed itself.

I moved from my 'Storybook Cottage' home in the mountains to the southern Gold Coast. Although the move began as a six-month sea change, it became permanent when I met Jen, who became the love of my life and we moved in together, then got married. Now I live in a love-and-light filled home.

In amongst that geographical change, my relationship with Mum ended. Full stop. She accused me of elder abuse at the end of 2021 and claimed our family property as her own, an accusation and action far too dangerous and deluded to ignore or deny.

After three intense years of caring for her wellbeing through the bushfire and its aftermath, then COVID lockdowns and her incessant demands for a campervan to go travelling in, it was too much to bear, particularly while helping to care for other family members during this time. When she took back the family property she had given to Cal and I 15 years earlier – the one we poured ourselves and our incomes into to maintain, renovate and in Cal's case rebuild after the bushfire – I walked away.

Alice knew what to do and that was initially, to draw a great big boundary around herself for protection. Then to forgive and release her mother's behaviour. But not to go back. Being accused of elder abuse is dangerous territory. Then to have one's home taken away, is beyond the pale. Alice, with the help of Jen, learned to let go, eventually leaning into that situation with growing equanimity.

Alice is starting again with vigour, enthusiasm and gratitude at having a second chance at life. At the age of 60, Alice is reigniting her passion for enterprise and service and taking to the world of business believing in her skills, experience and capacity to truly help people evolve their minds and lives.

At 60, Alice is tending to the garden of her love, intimacy and marriage with Jen.

At 60, with the deepest of connections to her grandchild, children and wife, Alice is also choosing to love herself. To nourish her tender heart and sometimes messy mind. She's accepting herself in all her light and shade.

At 60, Alice is surfing hard. You'll find her most early mornings, somewhere out in the waves of the southern Gold Coast, grinning like a maniac with her spirit burning bright. ◎

# The Queen of style

*Dedicated to my grandmother Helen Mant aka Nanny*

*On a day, two years to the day of the bushfire,*
*a day of pumping sou'easterly swell with*
*shearing walls of emerald water as big as buildings*
*stampeding to the right of the rock*
*I think of my grandmother.*
*In all this elemental wildness*
*I remember her pearl necklace –*
*shimmering marbles from the sea –*
*strung about her neck*
*with an intricate clasp connecting endings and beginnings.*
*Her cut-glass jewellery bowl and its perfectly fitting lid*
*hold pride of place on my shelf at home;*
*facets catching night-time light and*
*illuminating dark corners of my life.*

*We were the best of friends.*
*She was the Queen of Style at David Jones department store*
*And would take me there each holiday*
*cultivating my quirky taste for all things glam*
*while back at her place I would try her lipstick, perfume, scarves and cardigans,*
*forever exploring her fit-to-burst-at-the-seams wardrobe*
*of frocks and shoes with straps, gold buckles and little heels.*
*I journeyed in her orbit like a traveller to warm exotic lands.*

*I've inherited her sneeze – though not as exuberant or long,*
*a trail of puppy "tishus-tishus-tishus" followed by raucous giggles at*
*the way of it all.*
*Some genes are meant to be worn with mirth.*
*When she passed – in her 80s – at the tail end of a life fully lived*
*I dived into her wardrobe to bottle her smell*
*I wore her knitted rainbow jacket like the sun*
*I slept in her bed reliving her warmth.*
*I cried for years with the tears of yearning.*

*On a day, two years to the day of the bushfire*
*when so much of home was lost*
*on a day of pumping sou'easterly swell*
*with shearing walls of emerald water as big as buildings*
*stampeding to the right of the rock*
*I think of her.*

*My grandmother's hands are as soft as sweet pea petals.*
*I still hold them in my dreams.*

> **"** *Forgiveness is the letting go of hope for a better past* **"**
>
> Lee Holden

# Dear Dad

It's a long time since I last saw you.
I was only seven years old. That's over 50 years ago.

I have only a couple of clear childhood memories of you, of us.

I remember you holding me in the ocean in that big, wide, rough-and-wavy blue. We were out in deep water but you must have been tall enough to keep your feet on the sand so that you could also keep me safe in your arms. I remember feeling safe for that moment.

I also remember the day you took away my toddler pillow, my comforter called 'pilly' – to burn in the backyard fire with all the garden clippings. You thought I was too old to have such a baby thing. I must have been about three years old. I remember looking out the window with Mum, feeling agonised as smoke from the fire wafted high into the air. Then later you walked inside and gave back the pillow – intact – into my child's hands.

I don't think I ever trusted you again. That experience of betrayal wove its way through much of my life. You weren't to know how significant that moment was.

As I write to you, I'm now much older than you ever grew to be. What an astounding thought. You took your life so young – at 42 – after dealing with those demons of psychosis, schizophrenia no less, for so long.

I want to reassure you that no one else in our family inherited that disease. No one else is enduring what you endured in an era that seemed brutal towards people with such illnesses. Igniting fire was a thing for you wasn't it? I know you were institutionalised. Arrested. Institutionalised again. You lived through times when mental illness was poorly understood and those who lived with it were victimised, feared and separated from their community and family. I cannot for a second, imagine the terror and despair you must have sometimes felt.

To lose your family – your wife and two children – must have felt impossible at times. You never saw us again after we left and before you knew it, the courts strictly prohibited any contact between us because those were the days before 'No Fault Divorce' and you were deemed too dangerous to come near us.

I think by then, we were all wrecked. I feel sure I must have seen and heard things that no small child should ever see and hear, especially based on a few of the stories Mum told us about the last days of our family. Poor Mum. She gathered Cal and I up and escaped one day when our lives felt under threat. I'm grateful for her courage.

After we left, did you ever think about us? Did you ever wonder how we were and if we were growing strong and happy again? How did you feel about your actions and behaviour? Did you ever wonder if you could make things right again? Or did that illness keep taking you so far down that the only way out was a shotgun to the head? Alone in the world.

I'm thankful to your brother Sandy and his own wife and family for not only giving you a safe place to be when you needed that; but also for giving us – Mum, Cal and me – an unconditionally warm connection to the MacKinnon clan. They all treated us so kindly and we visited them regularly during school holidays. I think you would be grateful to them too because they loved us on your behalf.

Mum is still alive at 83 and I think at times in her life, she has missed you. She's not been able to say much about the marriage. She was so young, so naïve, so inexperienced. She had no idea what she was walking into. She's never remarried and only once, was she able to find intimacy with another man.

Dad, you have three incredible grandsons. Clancy and Mackie are Cal's sons and they're now in their late twenties and early thirties. They're both film-makers – Clancy can be found making documentaries

for the eco-activist organisation Sea Shepherd with his partner Ruby. He's done some Antarctic whale-protection missions; he's been to Mexico to document the protection of almost-extinct dolphins called the vaquita, and he's also been to Canada to work with First Nations people to protect wild salmon. Clancy is tall and hairy like a brilliant bear.

*Mackie and Clancy, my nephews*

Mackie makes beautiful surf films and is my favourite surfer in the world. He has such style and grace and has been surfing since he was about eight years old. When I took up surfing in mid-life, Mackie became my surfing mentor and inspiration. He still is.

Huon is my son with David, and is one of the kindest, gentlest, warm-hearted humans you could ever meet. I think you would love him dearly. He's in his mid-20s and is married to Sammy. They have a daughter now three years old, the beautiful Elizabeth Rose, or Ellie for short.

I have never seen a child surrounded by as much love as Ellie, Dad. Across three generations, it feels like our family calamity and grief has been overturned and Ellie is held by the most loving, grounded parents.

You're a great granddad! And I am a grandmother known as "Moomoo", a name that got its start in the Scottish version of Nana (Mamoo) and morphed.

Ellie's birth rekindled a deep friendship between Huon's dad David and I after a long and difficult divorce. We made a pact when Ellie was born, that we would always have each other's backs and always have an open-door of communication, so that we could be the best parents possible for Hu and Sammy.

I am married to Jen. She's a bold, bright, loud and proud lesbian who is brilliant at standing her ground for equality and justice. She's a supercharged businesswoman and a super-loving wife. She's given me a second, third and fourth chance at life after a few tough years and I'm relishing every moment. We go by the names Mrs Jen and Mrs Alice and our life together is filled with love in all its richness.

I'm a surfer, writer and mindfulness coach. When I discovered surfing it rocked my world. All that adaptation I'd done throughout my life, starting with you and Mum when I was small, was blown apart when I learned to surf and I felt its freedom and flow. I've now been surfing for fifteen years and will surf until I die.

I feel I carry the resilience of the 'Saltwater Women of Skye' as I call them, in my blood, Dad. I know that the Isle of Skye in Scotland is ancestral territory for the MacKinnons and that your cousin Eleanor lived her life there, continuing to speak Gaelic too. Cal visited her many years ago and loved her earthy humour and chain-smoking ways. Huon went to Scotland just a few years ago too and adores everything Scottish. He carries the MacKinnon name and tartan proudly.

And Cal, I must tell you about Cal. Would you believe, he is a mental health nurse at a Gold Coast hospital. He studied nursing late in life – through his early fifties and as that course unfolded, he found himself drawn inevitably towards mental health nursing even though it terrified him at the

*The MacKinnon clan celebrating at Jen's and my wedding*

same time. He specifically works with older people who are in crisis and he is a gifted and kind nurse. I asked him the other day, as we were paddling the kayak (Cal) and the stand-up paddle board (me) in Currumbin Creek, what he loves so much about mental health nursing.

"I love seeing people recover," he said as we drifted across the water of the creek.

"When they are admitted, they are in such a state of crisis you wonder how they will ever come good again. And yet, the hospital system, for all its faults, works for them and many of them heal. I love seeing them leave us with the hope that they will function well again in the community."

He added that in the people living with psychosis like bipolar or schizophrenia, he hears echoes of you – the good man with the hard illness; and he wonders at the complexity of the brain.

Dear Dad, Cal and I think and speak of you often. We are so sorry that your life was short and tragic. We wish you only love and peace and the comfort of knowing your family, filled with children, grandchildren and great grandchildren, are living our lives with meaning and purpose.

I love you. ◎

# Moving the planets

Has there ever been a time in
human history
when women have felt safe in the world?
Has there ever been a time when we knew
we weren't potential prey
to men's power
and anger
and fury
and their righteous sense of entitlement?
Has there ever been a time when
we were safe?

So the Feminine is Rising, is it...?
When we look for the signs
we see girls acing it in academia and
playing professional footy and
winning equal pay in pro surfing
but 10-year olds are assaulted on family holidays.
The murders of young women in Melbourne are chronic
and the stats for men's violence against women reflect a
tsunami of blood.

We – the women –
take every possible precaution and
we teach our daughters diligently.
We – the women –
stand together to tell our stories and
raise our banners in overhead protests.
We – the women –
applaud and thank the men who stand with us
who hear us, see us, love us and respect us
but sometimes the effort to teach them and coach them
exhausts us.

I like the story of a shaman
Deep Woman
who in circle and alone
with infinite skill and strength
begins to move the planets to realign.
I see her achingly turn the earth towards
The Great Mother and
I wonder if this is
perhaps
the only way to tip the balance and
restore order in the world?

# My mother is the real Doctor Who

It was when I watched her step off the Brisbane to Gold Coast train ten years ago,
after one of her overseas backpacking jaunts, that I realised my mother
was a sassy traveller of time and space.

She'd just walked part of the challenging and sacred Camino Pilgrims Trail in Spain. It was perhaps her fourth or fifth expedition there, and she was straight off an international flight and onto the train to come home. I was collecting her at Nerang railway station at about 10pm and as she alighted onto the platform I saw her before she saw me so she was entirely in her own world. At 73 years old she looked strong, confident, relaxed and completely happy in her world-travelling skin. This was her 'thing', to travel the world with a small backpack, wearing elastic-waisted rainbow pants, sturdy hiking boots and a jaunty red bandana tied loosely around her neck. She'd been doing this since her early 50s when she inherited enough money from her parents to travel freely whenever and wherever the wanderlust took her.

She'd stay in youth hostels mainly – with the under 30s generation – and make friends everywhere she went. She'd actively apply her special spiritual healing powers to anyone open to a type of psychic, intuitive process she'd learned in all manner of workshops and retreats over the years.

She had fans all around the world who adored her singular approach to life and travelling.

She refused to take a mobile phone overseas and for weeks and months on end, was out of contact and reach with Cal and I. Occasionally one of us would receive a random photo texted to us by a stranger who had encountered Mum on the trail. This was her way of letting us know that she was alive and kicking.

*I am and always will be the optimist.
The hoper of far-flung hopes, and the
dreamer of improbable dreams.*

11th Doctor Who

When I saw her step off the train that night in all her travelling rainbow glory, sans mobile phone and family cares, I knew for certain, she was the real Doctor Who.

Seriously, who doesn't love Doctor Who? That human-looking, 900-plus year-old alien has regenerated for 60 years since the show first screened in 1963 – the year of my birth. So many fabulous faces of Doctor Who have graced our television screens as they travelled to extraordinary galaxies and with devilish panache to save lives, worlds and sometimes the space-time continuum.

When the BBC series was radically revamped in the early 2000s, my son Huon became an all-time fan. Almost everything in our lives was focused on the Doctor – from weekly TV screenings and DVDs through to school pencil cases, woollen coats and hand-knitted scarves. Little did he know his grandmother was living out the autumn of her life as his beloved Doctor.

When Mum was home on our family property she would breathlessly tell Cal and I of her latest spaceship and alien encounters in our neck of the woods. Her life at home was filled with her spiritual and psychic studies, alien spotting and developing the plans and means for her next international foray. It was a far cry from her life as a young, single mum raising two children in the wake of a collapsed marriage to a man with severe mental illness.

I have to give her credit for giving birth to Cal and I, ensuring our safe escape from Dad's disintegration, connecting us closely into the arms of extended family, seeing us through school and university, and loving our own kids as we married and grew our families. She did all of that even as her own life-pendulum swung wildly between the sacrifices she felt she endured from family responsibilities and her far-fetched plans and dreams of freedom.

It was during my year of intense therapy after the bushfire, that I gained a clear perspective of the roller-coaster life Cal and I lived with the real Doctor Who.

When I was seven and Cal two, we escaped Dad's violence and chaos. When I was 10, Mum sent me away to boarding school. At 13, we were reunited when she and Cal moved to the Gold Coast where I was boarding and the blessings of being a day girl rained down upon me. When I was 17, Mum and Cal moved to Geelong where Mum became a boarding house matron. What the hell with the boarding schools and intentional family separations?

At times during my adulthood, inexplicably and ironically, there were extended and frustrating periods of living together as a family of three – Mum, Cal and me – in Sydney and on The Summit property. With the help of therapy, I finally came to see Mum's pattern of creating overbearing closeness, leading to annihilation of our needs in order to satisfy her overwhelming desire for freedom, which then led to abandonment as she disappeared into the ether. It had been going on throughout Cal's and my lives and had a huge effect not only my own patterns of thinking and behaviour but on Cal's too.

We know now from Family Attachment Theory, how vital consistent loving parental care is, particularly in the early years of childhood from zero to eight. Unfortunately Cal and I missed out on that consistency, and we continued to ride Mum's wild pendulum swings for most of our lives, both believing that it was just how family was, yet also sensing its dysfunctional destructiveness.

I have to admit that Cal and I mostly believed we were awful children to our mother. Everything about her seemed to come with a high emotional price and we never felt we were able to fully pay the high price to make her happy. Doctor Who may be a much-loved character on the screen but to be their child was often, impossibly difficult.

Despite Mum's troubling approach to family, it also proved to be one of her greatest gifts to me because when I became mother to Huon, I swore I would be my mother's polar opposite. No pendulum. Deep consistency, commitment, and connection to my family has been my hallmark – to Huon, my granddaughter Ellie and her mum Sammy, to Cal, and my nephews Clancy and Mackie.

About 15 years ago, in an immense act of generosity, Mum verbally gave The Summit property and the homes we were all living in with our children, to Cal and I. She was spending most of her time travelling and she could see how much we both loved and looked after the property. Her condition was that we paid the rates, insurances and all other expenses to maintain our homes and the property. She said the stamp duty was too expensive to formalise the gift by changing the names on the title of the property and we believed her and agreed to the arrangement. In hindsight of course, we should have gone together to the family solicitor to put the agreement in writing. Or Cal and I could have taken out a loan to pay the hefty stamp duty and have the title formally changed to include all three of our names on it – Mum's, Cal's and mine.

But we didn't. We trusted her word. We proceeded to pour our lives, labour and income into a property owned by another on the flimsy, verbal promise of a 'gift'. We mowed, gardened, painted, repaired, maintained, renovated, improved, delighted in, wrote about, and photographed that property and our homes. The commute down the windy, narrow road to work and surf beaches was hard yakka, but we revelled in the big sky, golden sunsets, south western cumulous and flame trees that lit up rainforest gullies with scarlet bells every November. We hosted Christmas gatherings, Easter gatherings, birthday gatherings, house concerts, parties and retreats at our homes.

*....when I became mother to Huon, I swore I would be my mother's polar opposite. No pendulum. Deep consistency, commitment, and connection to my family has been my hallmark.*

We waved Mum off on numerous international travels and when that became too arduous in her mid-70s, she bought a campervan and began to travel in time and space across Australia, again practising her unique form of healing with fellow travellers and expanding her fan base. Finally, as she crossed the threshold of 80, even campervanning became too much and I helped her sell her van and secure a small car so she could travel safely up-and-down Beechmont's mountain road.

The bushfire hit when she was housesitting in Brunswick Heads. Then COVID lockdowns descended and I secured her a cottage just up the road until Cal and Ash's house was rebuilt and her granny flat habitable again. I visited her every day and did and delivered her grocery shopping, trying in vain to help her understand that the whole world was at a standstill, borders were shut tight and everyone was sheltering in place. It could not have been a more difficult scenario for the real Doctor Who to understand. She was desperate to travel again and dreamed constantly of buying another campervan to set out in. A year later, she put a deposit on an $80,000 campervan and sought to reverse-mortgage our property to pay for it.

Our complicated and difficult situation did not end well. How could it when the shock and trauma of the fire followed by COVID lockdowns had taken their toll on all of us.

In mid-2021 I was in the throes of renting out my storybook cottage and making a sea change to the southern Gold Coast for a minimum of six months. Cal was finishing his nursing studies and applying for work at hospitals on the Gold Coast and Tweed Heads. His marriage to Ash had ended in the worst possible circumstances and he desperately needed a change of habitat, so was looking to rent his home in order to move to the coast for a while.

The only thing Mum wanted to do was travel in a campervan, so late that year, in desperation, I took out a loan to buy her a small van that she could trial for six months to see if travelling still worked for her. As a family, we worked out our arrangements together, informed the family solicitor and put it into action.

Within a month of course, it came apart at the seams with Mum accusing Cal and I of elder abuse. She took complete control of the property just before Christmas 2021. She handed the campervan to me with its $30,000 debt and moved back alone to the property.

Neither Cal nor I have seen our mother since December 2021. Though she didn't press charges in relation to elder abuse, with that threat continuing to hang over our heads, it's not appropriate or safe for us to be in contact with her.

The homes we renovated, re-built and loved are not ours. The home I raised my son in and painted weatherboard by weatherboard, is empty. Cal lost his home twice, once to bushfire and then to our mother. The beautiful two-acre rainforest property with its three dwellings – two homes and a granny flat – is listed for sale on a glossy real estate website. Mum is living in Cal's house while the property waits to be sold. We don't know what she intends to do when it sells.

Around the time all of these cards tumbled like some sort of Shakespearean tragedy, I met Jen. We live happily and lovingly in her home. The hobo dog is here too along with just a few of my favourite books, artworks and bits and pieces. Jen has been extraordinarily generous to welcome me into her life and her home and we are growing our lives together with love and commitment.

*One of the random overseas photos of Mum sent by a fellow traveller*

Cal is beginning to flourish in work and life though he endured 18 months of dark depression after he lost his home twice and his marriage too, within that impossible time. With the help of trusted friends, skilled psychotherapy and medication, he's on the other side and beginning to imagine a brighter future. He is saving a deposit to buy a one-bedroom apartment on the Gold Coast.

Life with the real Doctor Who has been wild ride. Over the past few years I have done the big therapeutic work to see, understand, manage and change the patterns it imprinted upon me.

Mum learned to live her life unapologetically on her terms. She still does. ◎

# Eye of the needle

*Like many of her generation*
*my mother learned to sew.*
*Deep within the marriage that broke her*
*she made matching dresses – mother-and-daughter designs*
*from patterns of calico, cotton, chaos and confusion,*
*fashioned to ward off the gun, the knife, the psychosis*
*lurking beneath and in her bed.*
*My seven-year old's frock of super-powered hypervigilance and*
*run-for-your-life exit strategies does not fit me anymore.*
*It constricts my heart and sharpens my sight and mind into*
*a one-pointed protective shield that fights off*
*potential madmen in the guise of partners who*
*might just take me down.*

*Today my lover, the one who has*
*stormed my barricades with their wisdom and wit and warrior ways,*
*(and below those a vulnerability fit to break open the most guarded of hearts),*
*gives me a t-shirt that declares "Power to the Peaceful" in*
*flowers and doves and broad capital letters.*
*Together we unpick the seven-year old's seams*
*loosening the weave with conscious care*
*aware that the threads spinning*
*across one life to another hold tenderness and hope.*
*For a moment I stand naked and we touch – he and I;*
*And we touch, she and I;*
*the man, the girl, the woman, the mother, the father, the now, now, now.*

*I slide the new t-shirt over my head,*
*my arms slip into sleeves and my torso is dressed.*
*She fits well this peace.*
*I smile and stretch into life.*

"

*Ends are not bad things, they just mean that something else is about to begin. And there are many things that don't really end, anyway, they just begin again in a new way.*

"

C. JoyBell C.

# Poppy's gift

Once upon a time I was married to a man.
I was married to David, a handsome man who made me laugh a lot.
A man who was outdoorsy, who loved sciency stuff, who was a gifted teacher.

For a while we were a golden couple. We had a baby we named after an ancient Tasmanian pine tree. We named our baby Huon.

When Huon was four, David and I separated and then we divorced.

I don't know where all the love went. I don't know why it got so complicated; why it got so scrambled. All hell broke loose and I had the chance, step-by-step, day-by-day, week-by-week, year-by-year, to learn how to live in a war zone where the battlegrounds were about Huon's home, his holidays, his school, even his surname.

I realised that war was a fact of life and that divorce was not the end of the matter.

David re-partnered with Susan and built a new family with her three beautiful daughters. Huon went from being an only child to the youngest of four in a busy, headstrong household.

And I created a stable, steady, long-term part-time home for my son in the midst of a war zone. It took

a lot of energy. I held onto a lot of fear for a long, long time.

When Huon turned 18 the war stopped. It simply stopped.

No more ambushes, no more threats. No more need to search frantically for truces or to draw lines in the sand. There was no more need to negotiate anything at all.

I was finally and entirely, free.

At eighteen, Huon proposed to his high school sweetheart Sammy and she said yes (thank goodness).

Just before Hu and Sammy married a few years later at the astonishing age of 21, David's marriage to Susan collapsed and for the first time in his adult life, he was without a partner.

David came to Hu and Sammy's wedding alone. I thought he was brave and courageous in that big celebration of youthful love. He was completely alone.

David and Huon shared a dog named Poppy for many years.

Almost from the time of our family's disintegration, through David's second family and during the era of war, tiny Poppy with her thick coat of Jack Russell hair and womble features, was a constant for David and Hu.

On family changeovers at respective homes in respective cars in difficult silences and with curt uncomfortable sentences, there was delightful Poppy, bouncing around with her acceptance of everyone.

As Hu grew up, Poppy grew old, until one day neither David nor Huon had the home to gently accommodate her in her old age. But I did.

And so the little old womble came to live with me, and Cal, my neighbours and I got to know her hilarious ways, crooked teeth and terrible breath for the last six endearing months of her life.

One day Poppy died quietly, peacefully and quickly in the arms of David at the local vet.

David was devastated, as we all were.

By chance, Huon, Sammy, David and I found ourselves gathered together on the afternoon of Poppy's passing – in the kitchen of Hu and Sammy's home. We were there to say goodbye to Poppy and help bury her in the backyard of suburban Moorooka.

We boiled the kettle and drank tea and told stories about Poppy from all the different households who had loved her. I heard many new stories about that funny little dog and learned how fully her life ran through the life of my son and his dad.

We laughed and we cried and then Hu and David – father and son together – buried that sweet old dog in a river of tears that must be a relief for men to release. Years of tears in a moment of farewelling the old family dog. Bless them all.

Later, as tea and grief softened and opened us, our conversation blossomed into yarning about how David and I had met and how we fell in love. I took the plunge first and told how I fell for David's uproarious sense of humour, the one my son has inherited and made his own.

David spoke of a young woman on a beach in an orange cossie that made his heart beat fast.

We laughed.

The kids cringed.

And David and I looked again at each other with kind eyes.

For the first time in 20 years we saw each other and at last we said goodbye. ◎

# Camelot

*In the reflection of Currumbin Creek's dawn,*
*cumulous falling at my feet*
*like overblown tea roses littering*
*the bridal threshold,*
*a pair of immaculate brahminy kites*
*beckon me into their chestnut and white light.*
*Stillness between us descends.*
*I, already prostrate on my paddle board,*
*bow my head in prayer, while they,*
*secure in their royal robes and tree throne*
*benignly gaze down upon my unholy face,*
*delivering a largesse of wild*
*to the fringes of the suburbs.*

*Standing again*
*I paddle downstream to where this creek meets the sea.*
*Brine clarifies and aquamarine rises through*
*drifting sand that gathers and runs in*
*miniature mountain ranges —*
*an aerial landscape submerged beneath*
*my board and wandering thoughts.*
*The story I am telling myself is that love is*
*a wild and intense ride.*
*Unexpected, again.*
*I steady my feet upon board and water*
*and lean into the outgoing flow.*

# Grandparenting

When my son Huon and his wife Sammy sent through the photos of
their daughter's birth, Elizabeth Rose (Ellie) looked like a beautiful
flower with her soft pink, handknitted beanie and rosebud mouth.
Her sleeping face was the most divine thing I had ever seen in my life.

She was born in Brisbane – a two-hour drive from Beechmont – during the first weeks of Australia's nation-wide COVID lockdown in March 2020 and hospital rules were draconian. There was no chance of being anywhere near her.

Still, my heart swelled and broke open with joy in the confines of my cottage in the mountains as I drank in those photos and realised I had become a grandparent. A grandmother! Only a month earlier I'd trained as a Rites of Passage facilitator – a highly emotional and significant experience – and now here I was crossing the threshold of grandparenthood at the age of 57. Incredible.

During her pregnancy, as the belly of my daughter-in-law Sammy expanded, like many expectant grandparents, I dreamed about the type of relationship I'd like to have with my first grandchild. I'd had such a wondrous connection with my own grandmother that I knew of the joys that could grow across two generations. Nanny had been my rock, my friend, my fashionista. I'd spent decades in her company and that of her friends and,

as the eldest grandchild, our relationship felt just a little bit more intimate and special than those she had with any other in the family.

So I dreamed big about my relationship with my granddaughter in-utero. I would teach her to surf. We would paddle out together, revelling in each other's love of the ocean and wave-riding skills. I would teach her qigong and we'd practice deep breathing and slow-motion martial artistry together. We'd explore a galaxy of books from her earliest months right through our lives and share the wonders of glittering words. We'd go bush-walking together and create vegie and flower gardens and I'd introduce her to the gifts and grace of Mother Nature.

I'd babysit when her parents were at work or on a date and we'd snuggle up together yarning, giggling, and breathing secrets.

Most blessed of all, we'd be integral to each other's lives and I'd be integral to an evolving family eco-system that included her, her parents, aunties

> **"** *Becoming a grandmother is wonderful.*
> *One moment you're just a mother.*
> *The next you are all-wise and prehistoric.* **"**
>
> Pam Brown

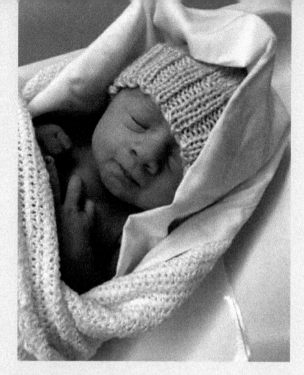

the lungs and digestive system *"because of a malfunction in the exocrine system that's responsible for producing saliva, sweat, tears and mucus. There is currently no cure.*

*"People with CF develop an abnormal amount of excessively thick and sticky mucus within the lungs, airways and the digestive system. This causes impairment of digestive functions of the pancreas and traps bacteria in the lungs resulting in recurrent infections, leading to irreversible damage. Lung failure is the major cause of death for someone with CF. From birth, a person with CF undergoes constant medical treatments and physiotherapy"* (Cystic Fibrosis Australia, cysticfibrosis.org.au)

(It's important to note here that since Ellie's birth, two 'miracle' CF drugs have come on to the market and are included in Australia's Pharmaceutical Benefits Scheme (PBS). This is an enormous help to the financial situation of people living with CF. They are known as Orkambi and Trikafta and are radically improving the quality and length of life for people of all ages who live with CF.)

Huon and Sammy became skilled at caring for a newborn with a colostomy bag – luckily Sammy is a nurse and a midwife – and after a few weeks, they were able to take Ellie home. Lockdown restrictions lifted enough for me to visit them all in Brisbane at least once a week taking care packages and endless adoration for tiny Ellie. Parents and grandparents alike, all found our family routines and rhythms and for five months, things unfolded gently, just like any other family with a new baby.

and uncles, and two other grandparents – Huon's dad David and Sammy's mum Lisa. I felt confident we'd work out how to share her amongst us.

On Ellie's second day of life she had a serious bowel operation and was diagnosed with Cystic Fibrosis (CF), the most common deadly disease in Australia. It was devastating.

Our kids and newborn granddaughter were physically unreachable in a hospital fortress at the start of a global pandemic which we knew bugger all about except it was respiratory. Cystic Fibrosis is a respiratory as well as a digestive system illness that is genetically inherited.

I dived into the Cystic Fibrosis Australia website to understand it. It describes CF as primarily affecting

One day when Ellie was six months old, she began to vomit. Suspicious, Hu and Sammy took her to hospital and then we all watched in horror as, over the course of a weekend, one by one her blood and kidney systems shut down.

Doctors and nurses scrambled to work out what was going on and how to save her life. After a fast-tracked diagnosis, we learned she also had an extremely rare genetic disease called Atypical Hemolytic Uremic Syndrome (aHUS). The US-based National Organisation for Rare Diseases (NORD) describes aHUS as an illness characterised by *"low levels of circulating red blood cells, low platelet count, and an inability of the kidneys to process waste products from the blood and excrete them into the urine. Severe high blood pressure and kidney failure are complications from this illness. Atypical HUS is a complex disorder and multiple factors, including certain genetic, environmental and immunological factors, all play a role in its development."*

Our Ellie was a unicorn – the Queensland Children's Hospital doctors had never before encountered a child with both CF and aHUS. They did an astonishing job in identifying it and saving her life.

Thankfully all of Ellie's treatments are registered on the PBS because in recent years, they have been among the most expensive medicines in the world to purchase. If not for the PBS, what would parents

do to save their child and give them an ongoing chance of a long, high-quality life?

After a nail-biting month in hospital, Ellie and her folks returned home again. They began to construct a life revolving around fortnightly hospital visits for aHUS infusions and to see the CF team for check-ins, physio, nebulisers, medication and vigilance. Remember, we're still in COVID lockdown land. The pandemic was morphing into different strains, the entire world was shut down, Australia's federation was in tatters as states closed borders against each other, and the global economy was in freefall. No COVID vaccinations, vax mandates or vax-related social/family divisions were yet on the horizon.

Ironically, in that tightly bubbled and locked-down world, dear Ellie and her family were at their safest because most people were being hypervigilant about germs and infection, there were no large gatherings and very little travel around the country or the world. As immediate family though, we were able to be in close face-to-face contact. We saw each other often and simply stuck to the COVID protection measures that the whole country was working with.

Huon and Sammy moved from Brisbane to be closer to Sammy's mum Lisa at Tamborine Mountain which also brought them nearer to my mountain home. We met for picnics, family celebrations and gatherings and, given the circumstances, we thrived. Grandparenting looked possible again and Huon even trained me in the basics of Ellie's care so I could potentially babysit if the need arose. It never really did, but at least we saw enough of each other for her to grow into knowing and loving her 'Moomoo'. Between her babyhood of late 2020 and second birthday in March 2022, we read and played and snuggled and giggled together often and in person. Ellie grew into a toddler with a huge open loving heart for her family and we all revelled (still do) in her fine company.

When Australia's state borders began to soften in December 2021 and the country prepared to open up again in the new year, in contrast, our family readied to lock down and create a tight bubble of safety around our little unicorn girl; as did families everywhere with immune-compromised loved ones. As the world celebrated its freedom in early 2022, ours and other families in similar positions created fortresses. And unfortunately, everything about my life excluded me from Ellie's bubble. I was by then, living on the Gold Coast, working in high-traffic public spaces and loving a conscientiously unvaccinated woman.

A year later in the lead up to Christmas 2022 I spent five days in isolation in a little rainforest cabin, so I was safe to see Ellie on Christmas Eve. It had been nine months – 270 days – since I had seen her in person at her second birthday, where her love for all things "Wiggles" was hilariously on display. We had stayed in touch by FaceTime all year and I'm eternally grateful for the technology that can help keep us connected. What a miracle it was to see each other's faces, read stories, play and laugh online.

Our in-person reunion on December 24 2022 though, was so emotionally moving it feels too special to write about. The touch of my granddaughter's arms around my neck when we hugged again was sublime.

My expectations and dreams of grandparenting had to radically change. Ellie is both immune-suppressed and living with CF, a combination that inexorably places her at risk not only from COVID but coughs, colds and flus. Maybe I could live a life more locked away and solitary but when I met Jen I chose intimate, romantic love, a vibrant community of friends, and vigorous, public work in the world. In doing so, I actually chose myself. I like living eight minutes from the beach and surfing every day. I love being with a great woman and having a big network of friends and colleagues. I value getting another crack at a career that builds on my education and experience, offers my services and care, and gives me a chance at financial success in the last third of my life.

*Perhaps becoming a grandparent is the ultimate journey of surrender?*

As grandparents, we have no control of our grandparenting destiny. All our hopes, dreams and expectations rest upon other's shoulders, needs, wants (and sometimes even whims). Our children and the partners they choose have their own hopes, dreams and expectations; their own lives to live in the best ways they know how. It's not for we grandparents to impose upon that. Some of us get the grandparenting dream; some of us get the nightmare; and some of us get left behind temporarily or permanently as we and our kids and their partners and our partners *all* make our life choices.

Perhaps becoming a grandparent is the ultimate journey of surrender? As grandparents, we feel the most unconditional love and adoration for our grandchildren but have no say in how they are raised or even when or how we get to see them. We learn to trust our children and honour them for their parenting journey; to defer to their own hard-won wisdom and in cases like Ellie's where a child has special needs, we thank all the gods that our kids are resilient, smart and vigilant.

I am hopeful that as Ellie grows older and stronger, her bubble becomes more inclusive. Indeed, as I write, we have had two brilliant summer beach days together in early 2023. At the same time, I'm relaxing my grip around some of those grandparenting dreams and learning to walk this tightrope of connection and care a little more graciously each day. ◎

# One year old

*A milestone this week.*
*She looks like an exuberant, concentrated*
*wind-up toy*
*miraculously coordinating*
*opposite arms and knees to propel herself*
*purposefully forward*
*shunting across the timber floor with a grin.*
*A delight of laughter ripples*
*through us all*
*as we witness her blossoming;*
*four months ago she was*
*fighting for her life*
*while we white-knuckled ours.*
*Now she is bonny and beautifully chubby*
*the only residue of the ordeal are our*
*overly tender hearts and*
*watchful, shining eyes.*

> *This is a wonderful day.*
> *I have never seen this one before.*

Maya Angelou

# Love

# The shed

It's the play of light and shadow across rippling roofing iron – now vertical as it is installed as external wall sheeting – that I see in my mind's eye when I remember the shed.

Shafts of sunlight captured and converted into art deco petals illuminating the morning from this unlikely structure that brought him back home.

He, is Cal, my brother and my closest friend. Five years my junior, we've shared this ride called life for so long I can barely remember a time without him. He has his own stories to tell and it's not my place to share them here; but in the fifteen years we looked after our homeland and mother at Beechmont together, the creation of the shed is perhaps our finest and certainly our most heartfelt moment.

There he was, tucked snugly into a loving relationship with Ash, who for a short while was also his wife; he was also a second-year nursing student, aged care worker, permaculture and flower gardener, avid photographer and parent to two grown men – Mackie and Clancy – when the fire struck.

He and Ash evacuated after I did that fateful Friday and it was Cal who texted me with the words "leaving now" at about 3pm. They stayed with a friend at Bangalow in Northern New South Wales while

I was with friends at Palm Beach on the Gold Coast. None of us could bear the sleepless intensity of staying in our cars near the Beechmont roundabout on that or the following nights.

When Cal and I reconnected at the first emergency community meeting on the Sunday after the fire, we had no idea his home had been destroyed. Neither did anyone else. So when we walked hand-in-hand under choking skies down the long driveway late that afternoon, to find it gone from the inside, we began a descent and recovery that felt almost Herculean in scale. It nearly took us down, each in our own ways, though we stuck together like glue throughout it all and we eventually emerged alive and kicking.

Post-fire, the construction of a small, temporarily-habitable shed for Cal to stay in whenever he wanted to be home on our land, became our anchor and our salvation. Crucially, it gave Cal a stable base, many months before the main house was re-built.

In the aftermath of the fire and a home burned beyond recognition, there were some grants available to those who had suffered great physical loss. With the help of such funding, Cal mapped out a plan to create a shed fashioned from mostly salvaged materials, built beside the big old heritage-listed macadamia tree in our shared backyard.

That macadamia tree. She was like the Mother Tree of our land with foliage so dense that on stinking hot summer days, her shade was the coolest place on the property to sit and rest.

The round, brown nuts she dropped with plonks to the ground, were a favourite of the raucous white cockatoos, perhaps the only birds with beaks strong enough to penetrate the armoured hulls and then devour the rich flesh deep inside.

Over the years, as we'd dash from one home to the other, shortcutting under the macadamia tree, we'd skate across the tree's marbles like crazed clowns, precariously balancing pot luck meals and baskets of goodies. I don't think either of us ever took a fall or lost a plate as we slid at speed from one home to another.

There was some roofing iron and a couple of big old timber-and-glass doors left unscathed from Cal's ruined home. A ramshackle farm shed already on the property, provided some heavy-duty as well as decorative posts. Our long-lost cousin Ross and his wife Hannah, owners of a Brisbane timber mill, read about our situation in a Courier Mail feature article

about the Beechmont fire, and they tracked us down and donated hundreds of dollars' worth of timber for the shed.

And Cal found Chris, one of the Timbarra neighbourhood locals with specialised skills in bespoke building construction. Chris, his wife Samantha and their young son Zephyr had also lost their home to the bushfire and as they waded through their own shocking losses, Chris seemed to find some purpose in our shed project.

Chris also had Tom, his offsider, a young bloke with a big heart for crafting special buildings from donated and salvaged timbers and quirky doors and windows. Tom was living with brain cancer. He'd already had a major operation though you'd never know it with his long, thick hair tied back in a pony tail, and strength enough to haul gear and fashion the shed bit by cumbersome bit. In the mornings when he'd arrive on the property and begin the day's work, his music would run to quirky jazz classics and alternative groove. After lunch as he tired, heavy metal would shriek across the lawn.

As the days and weeks of construction-by-feel wove into each other and the first wave of COVID lockdowns and isolation bit hard, Cal, Chris, Tom and I fell into a community of kindred spirits and kindness. Tom's ever-entertaining music became the soundtrack to our lives and our bruised hearts seemed to find peace in each other's companionship. Slowly the shed came together.

When the frame and flooring went up I'd wander over on weekend mornings to lie on the floorboards and gaze up into the sky and the edges of the macadamia tree, watching the unceasing activity of bird flight and clouds.

I was the only one living at the property at that point. I'd rescued Mum from potential heatstroke in the Brunswick Heads cabin she'd housesat through most of summer and had installed her in a rented cottage up the road. Cal and Ash were ten minutes further away in a rented house. I felt the strangeness of isolation and family separation during those days and nights because truly, what is a family property without a family to inhabit it?

*Isn't it strange the way one's memory of dates and months slips during shocking times?*

Isn't it strange the way one's memory of dates and months slips during shocking times? When I think back, I can only clearly remember September 2019 followed by the black summer of bushfires in early 2020. Then the first wave of COVID lockdowns descended in March/April 2020 before we'd even had a chance to begin to understand the gravity of losses from that firebrand spring and summer. The rest becomes a blur, though I sense that the shed was completed and ready for Cal around May 2020, just when autumn began to bite in the mountains.

I do, however, remember the happiness Cal and I both felt when he was able to set up a temporary home for himself in that carefully constructed, one-room building with its pocket-sized verandah jutting out to meet the mother macadamia tree.

And so, he came home.

Chris and Tom said their goodbyes and our small community of healing hearts reluctantly disbanded. (I called them back with their music and unique skills some months later to build the south deck and 'cloud mountain room' at my 'Storybook Cottage' thanks to COVID's early superannuation release scheme which gave me the funds to take on a renovation project that transformed my home.)

During that autumn and winter of 2020, Cal and I spent more time together than we ever had as adults – revelling in the beauty and wonders of our property. He'd bring his nursing books and computer to my place to study. Most early mornings we'd drink tea sitting in the sun on his tiny verandah. We shared homemade meals together at all times of the day and we began to reclaim the family in our property.

The joy I felt at his return was entirely uplifting and signalled our first decisive step towards repairing our lives. He began to gather together precious pieces of art and furniture and just as the shed had been built, bit-by-beautiful-bit, he began to build the beauty of his life again. A colourful cushion here with a comfy chair; there a bed with sweet dreams and a soft lamp. He even found a small puppy that he named Bene, short for Benediction, and Mackie, Cal's son came up to help him make a garden and a fenced area to keep dear Bene safe.

The shed also became Cal's safe haven when his dearest friend and former partner Jesse journeyed through her last weeks of life. Cocooned in the warmth of that single room through the dark days of winter, Cal was able to process the grief of Jesse's passing, safe in the knowledge he had a home again.

It's the play of light and shadows across rippling, vertical sheets of roofing-iron walls, that I see in my mind's eye when I remember the shed.

It's the joy of Cal's return to our homeland that I feel, alongside the great warmth of companionship, not only with my brother but with Chris and Tom too.

Chris and his family eventually sold their Timbarra property and have been adventuring around Australia. Sadly, Tom passed away in 2021. His passing was great loss to us all.

The shed stands strong. ◎

# When you think you have
# no more poetry inside

When you think you have no more poetry inside the light overflows with butterflies.
Paper aeroplaning, they drift
down the sky
with powder-fine
stained-glass wings,
coasting, gliding, dancing through thin air.
They swarm the dahlias, the marigolds,
and I,
crouched inside my garden,
whisper sweet nothings to entice them to my hair.
Japanese hand fans.
Dancing sunbeams.
Origami moments.
Blessings on the wing.
Tiny concertinas folding, unfolding
as they tiptoe across petals
en pointe.
Silent ballerinas dancing as we scramble to find our feet
on shifting ground.

# Landscapes of Love

The space is silent, dimly lit and cavernous with its slate grey floor and deep green walls rising like mossy rainforest ramparts. I enter. It's cool in here and light and shadows quiver and dance.

As I round the first corner, a creation story of monumental proportions surfaces and, stunned, shocked into stillness, I stand and weep, every sense stormed by this visually symphonic rendition of home.

This is celebrated landscape painter William Robinson's creation story painting of what we know as Binna Burra and Lamington National Park. His work is so visceral, so ethereal, so overflowing with the movement of light and life that I am instantly transported home even though I stand in the Home of the Arts (HOTA) art gallery just beyond the glitter of Surfers Paradise.

I feel the mountainous wind rushing up gullies of hoop pines and brush box – full-throttle gusting that turns the wheel of watery stars across creeks and crystal pools. The round moon reclines on a subterranean forest floor carpeted with fallen flame tree bells and leaf skeletons; a surface so soft with decay that I can walk soundlessly for miles like a monk in prayer in the temple of life.

Here is Gwongoorool Pool, the centrepiece, filled with stars and moon. Here is the track I walked a hundred times with friends and family in all seasons, in all weathers, year in, year out. Here is my toddler-son perched on my shoulders singing nursery rhymes as I sweat the three summer kilometres upwards after our midday swim deep inside the rainforest.

Here is the place I stole into first after the bushfire when the national park was still closed. Here, I clawed my way howling, through the tortured limbs of eucalypt giants charred beyond recognition until finally, finally the Coomera River revealed herself in an eternity of green and the wizened old eel welcomed me back into its fluid, ancient clarity.

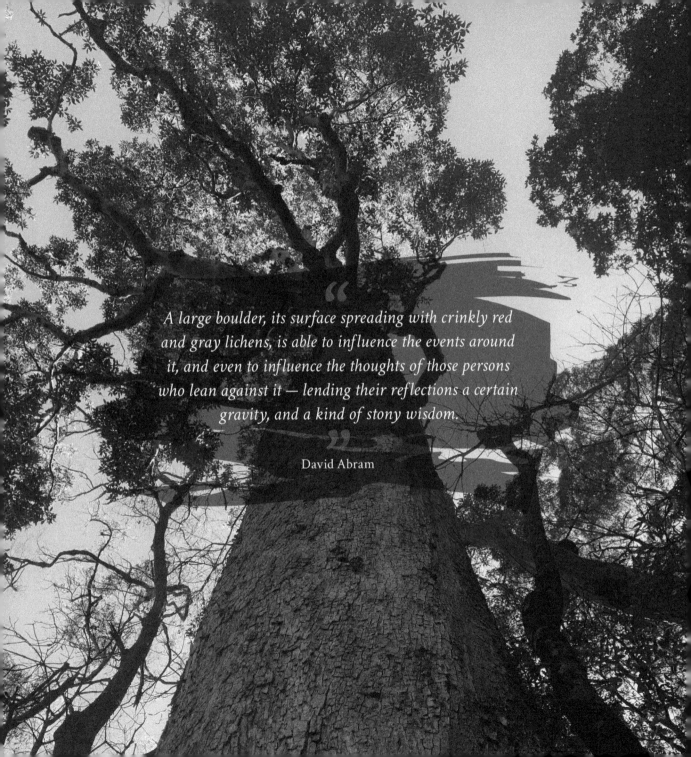

> *A large boulder, its surface spreading with crinkly red and gray lichens, is able to influence the events around it, and even to influence the thoughts of those persons who lean against it — lending their reflections a certain gravity, and a kind of stony wisdom.*

David Abram

My body is feeling every sigh of the Beechmont breezes, every whisper of the pre-dawn river of stars, every blink of the goggle-eyed tawny frog-mouth, every walk and every run and every foray I've ever made into that beloved, blessed rainforest.

My body holds all the feelings and stories I've been gathering since teenage-hood, when Mum, Cal and I began weekending at Binna Burra Lodge; swapping our suburban fibro cottage in Labrador for slab-timber sleeping, long communal dinner tables, rainforest jaunts and the smell of wood smoke.

In my mid-twenties in 1991, I moved to Beechmont permanently, and together with my then-husband David, raised our son Huon in that remote, spread-eagled community. A long time ago as I drove through Numinbah Valley – wedged with its upstanding boulders and shy creeks between Beechmont and Springbrook – I realised these landscapes are in my bones. While my ancestry is in Scotland, I am also of these mountains, valleys and rivers that rise in subtropical rainforests. My body is filled with memories, adventures and stories from these mountains that ripple to the sea, running in basalt ridges from freshwater to salt. This is the Wollumbin Bioregion, spinning around the ridges of the mountainous 'Cloud Gatherer's' shield – the 25-million-year old plug of an ancient volcano – that connects the Northern Rivers to Southeast Queensland. This is home.

I live in these landscapes and in turn, these landscapes live in me. There is a deep-running conversation between us – a practice I nourish – of awareness and devotion to this place and all life here. My mind reels at the depth of conversation that has attended to this place over millennia between the clans of the Yugambeh people, the Bundjalung people and the land; and the stories, in turn that this land herself holds…of humanity, volcanic evolution, epochal climate shifts, extreme weather…a landscape evolving in slow motion through deep time.

Might it be possible that as we pay attention to the landscapes that create layers of memories within our bodies, that the landscape herself is also paying attention and folding our presence in upon herself?

Could it be possible that the conversation is two-way and mutual? We know that the Earth – Gaia – is a complex, adaptive, self-regulating, infinitely intelligent living system. We know that we are swimming in a sea of energy (qi as ancient Chinese wisdom would have it) – internally and externally. Surely then, as our energies dance and converse at the most intimate and eternal scales, stories between human and landscape are born and honed and woven together over and over again.

In his astonishing article "*Storytelling and Wonder: on the rejuvenation of oral culture*", from the Alliance for Wild Ethics, deep ecologist David Abram speaks of the power of oral storytelling embedded in place. He writes,

*"...so much earthly savvy was carried in the old tales! And since, for our indigenous ancestors, there was no written medium in which to record and preserve the stories — since there were no written books — the surrounding landscape, itself, functioned as the primary mnemonic, or memory trigger, for preserving the oral tales... while the accumulated knowledge of our oral ancestors was carried in stories, the stories themselves were carried by the surrounding earth. The local landscape was alive with stories! Traveling through the terrain, one felt teachings and secrets sprouting from every nook and knoll, lurking under the rocks and waiting to swoop down from the trees. The wooden planks of one's old house would laugh and whine, now and then, when the wind leaned hard against them, and whispered wishes would pour from the windswept grasses. To the members of a traditionally oral culture, all things had the power of speech..."*
(Alliance for Wild Ethics, wildethics.org)

Over the past 15 to 20 years the fields of neuroscience and psychology have learned that our bodies and brains hold the memories of traumatic experiences, sometimes deeply affecting the way we interact and move through the world. As leading trauma neuroscientist and psychologist Bessel van der Kolk says, our bodies literally hold the score of our life experiences, particularly those involving trauma, particularly from our childhoods when the architecture of our brains was actively forming.

It is now clinically proven that there are techniques we can practice to notice the trauma-induced stories sleeping or buzzing within our bodies as well as the patterns of our brain function. Once we notice them, we can engage with our bodies, minds and nervous systems to soothe, converse with, recalibrate, express and even release them.

In the ancient movement and stillness practices of yoga and qigong, we understand that our bodies are run through with lines of energy that can be mindfully opened and moved using the breath and gentle movement.

These practices lean towards the notion that energy (especially emotional energy) can gridlock or stagnate in parts of the body like the hips, shoulders, neck and base of the skull for example; and that by moving our bodies and breathing deeply, slowly and with intent, we can help clear these blocks and re-open energy pathways to support health and longevity.

I wonder if there is a parallel between the way our bodies store our traumatic experiences and the way we gather and store memories and stories from within the landscapes we inhabit?

Surely over time, we must also lay down multiple experiences from nature like geological layers of sedimentation. The walks we make along rainforest tracks, the paddles we take along local rivers, the surfing of a handful of favourite beaches in all seasons, weathers, times of the day; year after year after year. Each time, with a new experience on the same track or at the same beach, the stories deepen and ripen. The memories, the stories are lived, leaned into, layered, one upon the other until our bodies become like libraries filled with shimmering stories of intimacy between ourselves and our local landscapes.

This is a conversation I am choosing to live into. This is the spiral of land, sea and sky come to life in my body which feels the cumulous rise in the south west corner of the afternoon sky after a day of summer scorch and subtropical humidity.

This is the story my heart sings at sunrise with the dawn chorus as a fresh day breaks across my life. This is the heart that explodes with ecstasy as I paddle my surfboard out at Currumbin Alley or Lennox Head, rising sun blaring like a loudspeaker in my face and urging me to dance across watery waves of energy that have travelled halfway around the earth to land on our local sandbanks.

My heart also holds a thousand breaks and cracks. It has rifts running through it every which way – ructions and earthquakes from love gone wrong and run amok: old partners, the annihilation and

*I wonder if there is a parallel between the way our bodies store our traumatic experiences and the way we gather and store memories and stories from within the landscapes we inhabit?*

absence of my parents, dream jobs that morph into nightmares, and the grief and sorrow of the rape and pillage of Mother Earth.

As I quietly weep in the cavernous rooms of HOTA, before the brilliance of William Robinson's creation stories, there also stands my heart, beating, beating; pumping blood, nutrients and oxygen around my body of stories.

Do your job, dear warrior heart, as you break and heal, break and heal, rewelding, rewilding yourself hand-in-hand with sunsets over the sea and mist seeping through rainforest. Remember dear heart, dear body. In these days of unknowing, it counts to remember, remake and re-tell our stories of place and people.

Remember. ◎

# Stream of consciousness

We paddle our boards against the falling tide the exhaling river
to skim wide-eyed across shoals and emerging reefs –
layers of sand, sediment, basalt and sandstone laid down
over eons, by yesterday's tides and the last big deluge.
I have been here before
with another lover.
This river is filled with memories of them, of us,
breathing in tandem
breathing in peace
breathing in silence
on the rising, shimmering tide, starry-eyed.
We found a beach here and when we pulled in to rest
we kissed, welcoming
sea air with its ephemeral salt into our mouths and across our lips.
This place is a stratum of sedimentary layers
a landscape of memories
made over months and years of paddling upstream
riding the tides
inhaling the mud of the river banks
which are sometimes bare
sometimes punctured with crab holes and ray divets
and sometimes submerged by a fluidity of Australian water colours:
tea tree
flooding mud
flooded gum
mangrove olive green
striking high tide crystal clear.

I inhale and exhale long and deep in the midst of this landscape

of love and loss.

I lean onto my paddle as it plunges into this stream of consciousness.

I breathe and feel my shoulders hold strong

my feet wide upon the board, balanced, supple,

brave legs buoyant.

I float, I dig, I propel, I smile

and this body, this river, this valley, this place –

all fold in upon each other.

A lifetime of memories merge.

The Old Ones, the Sentinels, now embodied in river rocks and boulders

nod in recognition.

> *I have always believed, and I still believe, that whatever good or bad fortune may come our way we can always give it meaning and transform it into something of value.*
>
> Hermann Hesse

# The last therapy session

Taking on therapy is no-one's idea of a fun time. Nevertheless, after a short foray into immediate post-fire therapy, a year later the symptoms of PTSD were still alive and kicking in my system.

So I sought out Mon, a trauma therapist on the Gold Coast and she agreed to take me on as a client.

Neither of us had any idea at the start, that our therapeutic relationship would last for a year and traverse not only the impacts of the bushfire, but also my early childhood and my relationship with my Mum and Dad.

I was, however, a diligent client through it all – journaling like a mad thing after each session and processing day-by-day as I sought to reclaim my life.

It was, all in all, a gruelling experience and one I would not change for the world. I still think of Mon with deep gratitude almost every day. By the time we decided I had had my last official therapy session we were in complete agreement that I was ready to head out into the world feeling integrated and wholehearted. That felt like some sort of miracle given all we had peeled back, eyeballed and worked our way through.

Just before our final session, I had hosted and facilitated a relaxation and yoga retreat at Beechmont. That in itself felt like redemption because post-fire, despite all my years of retreat facilitation, I was sure I'd never have the inner grace and spaciousness to work with people in that way again. Yet there I was, on a Sunday in October 2021 diving deep with a warm group of people and holding them safely and kindly.

At that last therapy session with Mon, I told her about teaching gentle yoga at that retreat and how soothing it felt for our nervous systems. I told her I sensed an ability within me, to take people into deep calmness and peace through practices like qigong, yoga, yoga nidra, savasana and meditation. I told her it felt like my gift.

And Mon said a profound thing. She said because I had felt and lived through huge chaos during my life, with all the help of our therapeutic work of reflecting, observing, journeying, and integrating – I now had the capacity to feel the polar opposite of that deep chaos, which is deep calm. She said if I hadn't felt those depths of chaos I wouldn't be able to feel the depths of calm, or to offer others access to that.

In that moment, Mon gave me the gift of *meaning*. She gave meaning to all I had lived through and endured, and to all the work I'd done to heal, particularly over that whole gnarly year of therapy with her.

I have found the deepest of calmness out of the deepest of chaos. And I continue to practice – mindfully and consciously – that peace and calmness every day. I subscribe to the notion of 'living as a practice', where daily life offers unlimited opportunities to practice peace and emotional self-regulation no matter the circumstances.

*I have found the deepest of calmness out of the deepest of chaos. And I continue to practice – mindfully and consciously – that peace and calmness every day.*

It is a central value to me and is entirely wrapped up in the process of healing and recovery I gave myself to.

In our many sessions Mon and I covered a lifetime of reflection, and together we defused and stored trauma safely. At our last session she had Bessel van der Kolk's book *"The Body Keeps the Score"* on her desk and that seemed entirely appropriate. It was probably five years earlier that I'd read that book and every lightbulb in my head switched on. That was when I began to deepen my journey into my family history.

Who knew that a bushfire would, a few years later, connect into and explode that history to catalyse an urgency of healing? Who knew that I would actively and thoroughly untangle so many of the knots that were holding me prisoner?

But by the end of the year of therapy I felt largely untangled. I became conscious and mindful of the patterns of thinking and behaviour that were gouged into my system in my early childhood. Once I was capable of noticing them I could, and did, and continue to, work actively and consciously with them – as a mindfulness martial artist.

What a gift to become capable of intimacy, love, compassion, steadiness, stillness, deep calm and deep happiness. ◎

# For Jen

*We meet in the sea.*
*She with her quiver of rainbows*
*spearheading bold goals for herself and all women*
*me with a heart wide open and ready to fall for love –*
*her love.*
*We are brought full circle,*
*back to our childhood dreams of starry starry nights, storytelling and*
*happy endings.*

> **"**
> *Cut the ending. Revise the script.*
> *The man of her dreams is a girl.*
> **"**
>
> Julie Anne Peters

# My dream man is a woman

I decisively jumped the fence at the age of 57.

After a life of heterosexuality, in mid-2020 during the first round of the COVID pandemic, I met a transgender man and we fell into each other's arms, beds and lives in a blistering love affair that took me to the heart of the LGBTQI or Queer world. Though it burned out nine months later, what that super-charged relationship gave me was the depth of emotional connection, physicality, sexuality and companionship that I had always dreamed of. I knew I would never return to the straight world of relationships.

I know I'm a late bloomer but in all honesty, 57 seems to be pushing things to their limit don't you think?

Yet today, as I craft the sweetest intimacy and love with my new wife Jen, I am standing tall and strong in a world of delight that I am so glad arrived late in life.

If the truth be told, I spent most of my adult life believing I was a failure at intimacy and romantic love. It began in my late teens when I sabotaged the naive love blossoming between my first boyfriend and me. Having been raised by a single mother after surviving a chaotic early childhood I had no idea how to be safely vulnerable when sharing my heart with another.

I lost my virginity to a delightful Englishman at 21, an age that seemed horribly tardy in the era of 'puberty blues' when many of my contemporaries started having sex at 14 or 15.

There was a ten-year marriage to David that birthed the love of our lives – our son Huon. After our divorce there were other men and some significant affairs of the heart. An engineer with four children, an activist musician, a surfer, a postie, a developer with a social conscience…all decent men and none of them ever violent or abusive.

I spent decades wandering the maze of heterosexuality, never really questioning it but never really finding my mojo with the men I dated, loved, married and lost.

And I kept waiting for my dream man to show up.

You know, the one who was sporty, emotionally intelligent, good looking, witty, tender, vulnerable and strong. The one who loved poetry, writing and surfing too. Yeah, that one.

I felt I should be one of the lucky ones and yet I stumbled and fell in every single relationship; never feeling fully heard or seen. Not even feeling *partly* heard or seen. Instead, I did a lot of hearing and seeing of endless opinions and mansplaining until each time I simply couldn't hold the early sweetness, and cracked. Either they left or I did, hearts hurting, egos bruised, minds churning.

I didn't realise in this crumbling landscape of love that my early childhood trauma was also running amok. All of my Dad's schizophrenic chaos and violence hurled at Mum meant my five-year old child-self encountered situations one would never wish upon our worst enemies. My developing nervous system and brain found ways to cope back then and in turn, imprinted themselves on my long-term behaviour patterns and hitched a ride into adulthood and the visceral give-and-take of intimacy. As a result, I always had exit strategies at my fingertips and used them at the first sign of trouble.

In October 2021 after a quick stint of online lesbian dating, I reached out for Jen, a Gold Coast surfer I sometimes crossed paths with at my local break. She's a bold, proudly out, surfing lesbian with a smile that lights up the beach at sunrise. In a fit of courage I asked her out on a surfing date with a cuppa and a yarn afterwards.

She graciously accepted and we connected for so much more than the quick nod we'd enacted for years as we'd passed each other in the water.

Jen knew she was a lesbian early – from her late teens-early twenties. She lived out and proud through the hard-edged 1980s and 90s when lesbians were run out of the armed forces and publicly derided. Back in those days, same sex marriage was entirely out of reach and lesbians, gay men and transgender people endured unimaginable discrimination.

Jen is one of the kindest, most unconditionally generous people I have ever met. She's a savvy, successful entrepreneur and philanthropist. She's spunky, sporty, funny, emotionally intelligent; a writer, public speaker, podcaster, and surfer. *She's a surfer!*

She's also an indefatigable champion of women's empowerment with a deep knowledge and appreciation of the suffragettes and the history of lesbianism through the ages. She tells me that it's not unusual for older women to jump the fence in their 50s, 60s and older. This is a time in our lives when we often become more comfortable in our skin, unapologetic about our life choices, and a little bit (or a lot) fearless about our sexuality.

In the early days of our relationship we focused on being present and mindful with each other. We consciously harnessed the wild horses and monkeys of the mind that can race ahead and worry about figments of the imagination or the past. We revelled in each other's company.

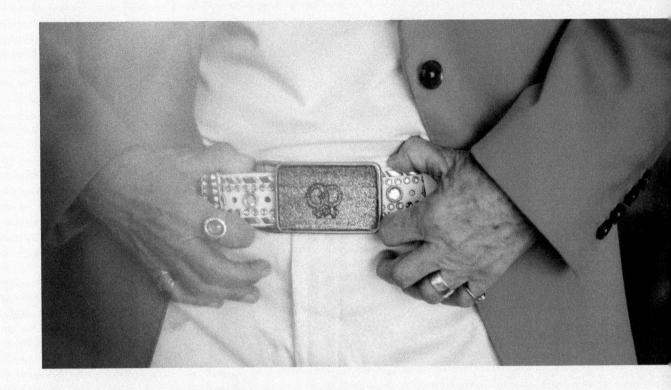

We surfed together almost every day. We walked along the beach holding hands, speaking deeply of our lives and histories. We cuddled and touched and kissed and laughed loudly and had great sex. We didn't hold much back; not in public, not in private.

I felt entirely relaxed and supremely happy in Jen's fine company and when she proposed marriage to me two months into our relationship I gave her an emphatic *Yes* after being completely taken by surprise.

From the very beginning we knew how to teach each other good stuff, listen deeply and support each other openly and joyfully.

The process of coming out in my late 50s, and of walking mindfully and openly into the lesbian and queer world was entirely liberating. Its synchronisation with effective therapy and the practice of much-needed relationship skills was life affirming.

I feel great happiness in announcing to the world that my dream man is a woman as Jen and I walk the path of crafting enduring love. ◎

# The harvest starts

Bursting through brown soil,
the vine strung with flowers lights up this rainy day
with smiles as bright as the sun.
Their gowns are classic yellow –
I can almost taste their honesty and hear them sing as
they hang about on the old timber fence
not climbing, but reclining,
a profusion of tiny cucumbers in the making.

It's been a month of life-changing confusion.
So many rugs yanked out from under my feet
I'm shocked I'm standing at all.
But here is this house,
only newly a home and
Jen is building the soil for a mighty harvest a year from now.
I hold strong and prepare.
Our bed is made
and turning the bitter old wives' tale on its head
we lie in it with delight
learning each other's bodies and ways and cultivating
the seasons of the heart.

I aspire to the witchery of healing plants and she calls up the crones,
reclaiming the wisdom, wit, wiles and wonders of women
who no longer bleed and instead,
make their lives anew.
There's no room here for fence sitters or wallflowers
Look out! There are warriors about
no longer making prisoners of their hearts, but
setting
each other
free.

On this dripping rainy day,
a blessed break from summer's relentless light,
she plants a food forest in my heart and the newly mulched beds.
Cucumber flowers flourish by the fence,
not climbing but reclining in their fresh yellow gowns
that tell us the harvest has begun.

*Love is our true destiny.*
*We do not find the meaning*
*of life by ourselves alone*
*– we find it with another.*

Thomas Merton

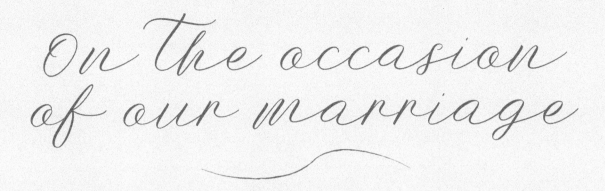

# On the occasion of our marriage

To my darling wife Jen...

Our love story began the day I saw the film "*Supernova*". I was with someone else then, but I knew they didn't want the committed "till death do us part" relationship heartbreakingly portrayed in that film. I realised that I did. And from the moment the last notes of that film played out, I started to search for you.

Ironically, I think you would hate that film. Its slow metronome pace is at odds with the speed you live your life, watch your films and listen to your audio books. I don't even like audio books, let alone played at double speed. Nevertheless, the deep love and commitment of the couple in that film, played so poignantly by Stanley Tucci and Colin Firth, captured my heart and I knew beyond a shadow of a doubt, I would *not* live out the rest of my life alone.

I reached out to you in October 2021 after five years of passing each other at the beach as we entered and departed the surf. We were Facebook friends and I always found your online presence unashamedly bold, bright and authentic. You were out, loud and proud. Your purple jeep resplendent with rainbows and unicorns was unmissable – it's a local landmark really. For a long time I didn't know what to make of you except deep down I also thought you were a fucking spunk and so I was drawn inevitably into your orbit.

The day I invited you out for a surf and a cuppa was the day I realised you would *never* recognise I had jumped the fence sexually. To you, I was just a good Queer ally and a slightly aloof surf instructor. I didn't know if you were single, dating, or in a relationship; I just knew that if I didn't make the first move, no moves would ever be made between us.

And you responded immediately on one of the toughest days of your life.

You were available! Unattached! The playing field was clear and uncomplicated! We had our first date two days later – in a rough and tumble surf, onshore wind and north east swell, followed by brekkie, a long yarn and a close embrace. It took two weeks to kiss and again, I was the one who muscled up the courage to do the asking. Really?! The newbie to the same sex relationship world stepped up again to invite the long-time butch dyke to kiss!

Sex was even longer coming but all that space gave us time to talk and surf and connect and laugh and for our hearts to open and be brave and soft and whole all at the same time.

Don't ask me why I didn't respond to your personal message five years earlier. I really don't know why except, perhaps, way back then you were too big and bold for me and I hadn't stepped fully into my own skin. There was much ground to cover between your original message and my response five years later.

Dearest Jen, I love everything about you from the top of your head to the inside of your tummy. You hold nothing back, living life *big* and on your terms but still with respect for others and how they choose to live. That's inspiring.

You are the most wholeheartedly generous person I've ever known. You give your time, love, energy, knowledge, wisdom, laughter, friendship and material support unconditionally. My goodness, look at the not-for-profit, Q Foundation that you established ten years ago to enable children in Thailand to gain an education, nutrition and family support. Even through the financial freefall of COVID, you kept all those kids and their families going.

You are a deeply spiritual person, integrating your practices into everyday groundedness; a rare and precious thing.

I love that at 62, you are a frothing grom surfer, like a 10-year old boy new to the wonders of the water. I love that our passions for the ocean, surfing and sunrise are perfectly matched so there's never any apologising for long, dawn surf sessions. Quite the opposite. I love that our life together is grounded in surfing.

I love your big sense of humour and joy of laughing. I love the way you've rediscovered your inner child and channel her into hilarity, play, fairy lights, rainbows, unicorns, sparkles and whimsy.

You are completely and utterly consistent in your love and respect for me. That's unbelievably healing after a lifetime of wild pendulum swings between overbearing saccharine sweetness and abandonment in family patterns. Experiencing that consistency with you makes my life shine and I have never ever felt so safe.

You also have great hair, glorious cheekbones, beautiful eyes, luscious lips, silky skin, awesome quads, hamstrings and shoulders. And you're damn handsome too.

When you asked me to marry you two months in, my head spun out and my gut yelled 'Yes!' The housewarming do became the engagement do, and you gave me the rose quartz ring as a symbol of your constant love. Never have you wavered.

How was that wedding day of ours, babe? Never have I felt such joyous community. We all lifted the roof off Mo's Desert Clubhouse with our love, laughter and tears of happiness. One big family filled with grace and hope; yes, hope that there really are happy endings in this crazy-weird world.

As you know so well my love, when we commit to catching a wave in the surf, we give our whole selves to that process. We choose where we look (never down), we match the wave's speed, paddle hard and align ourselves with the energy of *that* wave and *that* moment. We also remember to breathe. We give ourselves over to a force that's much bigger than us.

In my commitment in marrying you Jennifer Jefferies, I consciously align myself to the energy and momentum of our union, which is so much bigger than either of us as individuals. Paddling into it, I bring my attention to nourishing the big and the small things that in turn nourish a healthy home and a healthy 'us'. I give myself wholeheartedly to paying attention and nourishing us for the long term because I believe in you and me and us. I believe in what we have and I believe that what we're continuing to cultivate, tend and grow is worthy of my full attention and energy. This is the most beautiful, big, long wave I could ever hope to ride.

Being married to you is a living statement of our love, respect and commitment to each other. It's also a monumental way to celebrate the beauty of love. And it's a deep bow to your courage and commitment to gay rights throughout your entire

adult life. I respect all that you and the Queer community have done to legalise same sex marriage. This is personal and it's political; it's respectful and loving in every way.

I love you now and forever,

Your Alice.

# Tea rose

*The tea rose spills her scent across the white bench.*

*Soft orange (or is that apricot) as*

*tight buds blossom and petals unfurl,*

*layers and curls*

*in a Georgian waltz,*

*dance cards filled with flirting.*

*Our life together in this house of summer light and*

*white plantation shutters, is*

*woven through with tendrils of perfume and laughter,*

*daily green waves and surf reports,*

*big community and the*

*vast horizons of love.*

*Our world unfurls to the rhythm of roses and tides and*

*atmospheric lows and highs.*

*Through all weathers*

*we blossom.*

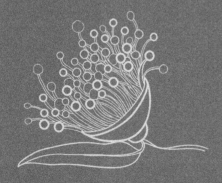

> **"**
> *Courage doesn't mean you don't get afraid.*
> *Courage means you don't let fear stop you.*
> **"**
>
> Bethany Hamilton

# Water

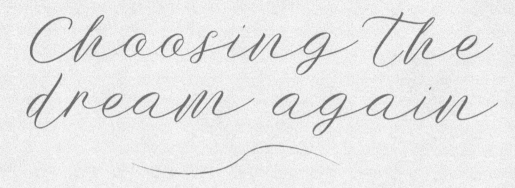

# Choosing the dream again

Until recently, I'd lived most of my life believing I lacked courage.
Ashamed of my lack of courage. Let me explain.

As you know dear reader, I spent the first seven years of my life in a family that was king hit by schizophrenia and domestic violence.

I don't remember any details but in conversations with my brother and mother a few years ago, I learned enough to understand how desperately helpless and terrified small children feel when they can do nothing to protect the people they love.

That was my Ground Zero.

As a teenager growing up on the Gold Coast, Australia's surfing and holiday playground, I seemed from the outside like a typical beachy, sunshiny teen.

But every day I felt a million butterflies swarming through my belly. I worried about everything: fitting in, following the rules, getting good grades, making it into sports teams, finding and keeping friends, my family surviving financially.

Disasters and catastrophes lurked around every corner.

As a teenager though, I also *really* wanted to surf.

When I grew up on the Gold Coast during the 1970s and 80s, the era of the shortboard – fast, shredding, three-finned thrusters – blazed its way into our community. These boards revolutionised surfing and at the same time, most guys who rode them seemed to hate women being out in the water with a vengeance.

This era was also before the birth of surf schools; so if you were a woman who wanted to surf, you had to figure things out yourself in an environment that was brutally unforgiving and fuelled by the worst of Aussie testosterone. To me it was the age of rage.

I tried surfing a few times on garage sale boards I'd bought. I'd get down to the beach, wax them up and hit the water over and over again. Face first. Backwards. In squealing catapulting cartwheels. Those surfboards seemed to have a mind of their own. Even the smallest waves felt intimidating and there was no one to give me even a crumb of advice. Out the back the guys ruled and the gates to that kingdom were locked fast against young women like me.

Eventually I gave up.

By the time I was married and had a baby, the dream of surfing was gone. My life revolved around learning how to be a wife and mother and how to save the Earth as a professional environmentalist and community volunteer.

Then there was divorce, shared parenting, fear about being a sole income earner, even amid saving the Earth and community volunteering. I sacrificed sleep to keep all those balls in the air. Life was frantic.

The saving grace was an annual two-week camping holiday by the beach at Lennox with just me and my son Huon. There were no TVs, no computers, few responsibilities and I barely ever looked at the mobile phone. I was usually the first one on the beach at dawn and the last one to leave at dusk. It was bliss.

Fifteen years ago, on one of those holidays, right on the eve of my 46th birthday, I saw a learn-to-surf flier in the campsite laundry. After checking with Hu, I booked us in for three surf lessons – mostly for him of course. I was tagging along to keep him company.

Brett our instructor was a young, local surfer and a nurse with a friendly, warm and encouraging manner. Our first lesson began as we hauled our huge foam boards across the sand towards the water and Brett talked about how waves formed and broke.

I was already in love. Then we entered the water.

Waist-deep in the whitewater runners of Lennox, we turned our huge boards towards the shore and caught our first waves, lying on our bellies and paddling our arms like windmills. At that moment, as I paddled for my first wave, I experienced a blinding choice: to joke and muck about or to let that dream of surfing rise back up and give it life. I chose the dream.

Battered and neglected, the dream was still lodged deep inside me patiently waiting. So when I scrambled to my feet on my huge board on one of my first waves, instead of squealing and falling about like a middle-aged woman learning to surf, I focused and balanced and I felt that wave lift me towards the shore. My spirits soared and the Surf Gods shouted at last, *"You will be a surfer!"*

Huon and I had our three beginner's lessons. I celebrated my birthday. Brett the surf instructor lent me one of those huge foam boards for the rest of the holiday and I spent every moment in the whitewater of Lennox surfing. I borrowed a pair of Hu's boardshorts and a rashie and I practiced morning, noon and night (even in my dreams). I was absorbed. Enamoured. Unstoppable.

Now I'm not talking here about learning a sport or even taking up a recreational activity. I'm talking about a full-bodied, no-holds-barred spiritual awakening. A born-again conversion if you will, where I saw the light and the light was surfing.

Yes, it included learning how to stand up on a surfboard. Yes, it included learning how to paddle out through the shorebreak to catch waves out the back. But it was mainly about reclaiming my spirit and soul and the grand and passionate love affair I have always had with Mother Earth, Mother Nature and the ocean.

Surfing re-ignited the Wild Inside that had been lost to an adapted life. When I reclaimed that Wild Inside there was no going back. Ever.

I overturned my work life and walked away from 24 years of intense environmental activism. I re-trained and re-invented myself as a fitness coach, yoga teacher, qigong instructor and incredibly, a surfing instructor at the age of 50.

I saw Huon through his last year of high school. When he left our mountain home for Brisbane at 17, I threw myself into a life revolving around surfing and other mindfulness practices including meditation and Zen.

Like most of us I had bills to pay, a home to maintain, work to turn up to and clients to tend.

*Surfing re-ignited the Wild Inside that had been lost to an adapted life. When I reclaimed that Wild Inside there was no going back. Ever.*

But surfing took me into a life that is overwhelmingly filled with joy, playfulness, laughter, gratitude and devotion. It's a life fuelled by beauty, patience, grace and yes, courage.

Courage, because when I paddle into a wave, I connect to energy. BIG ENERGY. When I harness myself to that energy and surrender to it, I fly.

Courage because I've learned to trust again. I trust my board. I know her fins and rails will hold into the face of the wave. I trust my body. I know my feet will find the deck of the board fast and my legs are strong enough. I trust my mind. I know my breath will take me into crystal clear composure no matter what the conditions in the water.

So here's the kicker about courage. For a long time I felt embarrassed about my surfing story and hardly ever spoke of it. I thought I was a failure because I hadn't toughed it out in the 1970s and 80s to teach myself to surf in that aggressive male-dominated culture.

But one day at a women's soul surfing retreat, my friend and professional surfer Lauren Hill asked me to tell my surfing story. Reluctantly I blurted it out and her amazement and support transformed my feelings of shame into excitement. I realised I might have an interesting story that was perhaps worth telling more publicly one day.

In 2018, I wrote out my story as a book called *"Surfing as a Dance: How one woman found grace in and out of the water"* and with the help of three incredible women, it was published in December that year.

It tells my story vulnerably and courageously. From that early childhood of terror to that first surf lesson and beyond, that book tells my story.

Because of surfing and writing that book, these days I stand tall, fierce and courageous. I am a changed woman who carries the Wild Inside like a warrior. I stand as a Warrior of Grace for the Great Mother, Mother Earth, and all women.

I tell my story for the women I taught to surf. I tell my story for the women who inspire and motivate me. I tell my story for my wife, my brother, my granddaughter and I tell it for you dear reader.

And mostly I tell my story for the little seven-year old girl who was lost for so long, then found through surfing. Who paddles out with me every day and who shouts her love for the world out loud. ◎

# the liminal zone

we're in it now.
molten skies – copper, bronze and gold –
the sun streaks west like a meteor
exploding.
satin sheets of liquid sea, slide
across our feet, our knees, and
though the swell is small
those beach-break runners
draw us inevitably into our psychedelic souls
not sure what's up or down, near or far, in or out.

we are at the mercy of the alchemist
turning stone into gold;
our crucible is the evening ocean.
we stay beyond the time of safety
addicted to the light, and then –
it's gone.
the day flickers, sputters, glowers
and we, under veiled new moon
start to study the deepening sea beneath our boards
our feet
for shadows.

one blink and it's all shades of grey and bottle-green
camoflage,
even the horizon is disguised.
our eyes adjust achingly slowly and
imperceptible lumps
become mounds
become peaks
become waves
which we feel our way into,
leaning into the liminal zone –
the place so close to heaven that if you stretch
your arm, your hand
you're there,
holding the lost love of those already gone.
the ones we howl for are here
in the hush and the sigh of ocean evening merging
into night.

*Piglet noticed that even though he had a very Small Heart, it could hold a rather large amount of Gratitude.*

A.A. Milne

# Like the tide
# we fall
# then rise

This story was written just a few months before the Beechmont-Binna Burra bushfire in mid-2019. It speaks with love about some of the women I taught to surf during the six years I was a surf instructor in my 50s, working at Currumbin Alley on the southern Gold Coast. During the first round of COVID lockdowns in 2020 when the whole world slowed down, I realised how exhausted I felt and I realised that surf instructing contributed greatly to that exhaustion. Keeping people safe in the crowded Alley waves, giving them fun experiences in the water, and helping them evolve their surfing skills was a challenging job description! During that lockdown I decided to finish instructing others and enjoy more time for my own free surfing.

However, the call to nourishing women (particularly women over 50), in and out of the water is strong. As this book goes to print in mid-2023, I am actively working with my wife Jen on two exceptional projects that aim to uplift women in their lives. The first is Smart Sassy Seniors – a weekly podcast and live events that help women of all ages live their lives more bold, bright and vital. You can find our podcast at *www.smartsassyseniors.com*

The second is the homegrown documentary "Taking Off: Tales of Older Women Who Surf", which Jen and I are producing with surf photographer Hannah Jessup and the Surf Witches Board Riders Club. Not only does this groundbreaking film showcase the stories of six women aged 59 to 72 years old, who surf the beaches of the Gold Coast, it also uses surfing as a metaphor to encourage older women to go after their dreams wherever they are and whatever their age. The documentary can be found at *www.takingoffdoco.com*

Here is a story about some of my wonderful surfing students written with love and joy for our community of women who surf...

The road is greasy with rain.

It's dark.

It's the deep dark of pre-dawn darkness that creeps close and breathes through the scarf wound round my neck.

Toc-toc. Toc-toc. Toc-toc. The windscreen wipers hold the comfort of a heartbeat, keeping the rain at bay so I can see my yellow headlights hit the bitumen.

I've been up since 3.30am; sipping tea, munching toast, journaling and meditating. Now it's just after five, and I'm driving my surf van down the mountain in late-season rain with two surfboards, 10 wetsuits and a ridiculous number of bikinis.

It takes an hour to get to the beach for this typical Wednesday dawn surf session with a community of mostly middle-aged women. I make this pre-dawn pilgrimage from my mountain home to the beach many times a week, both to teach surfing and to free-surf for myself.

In my crew there's Sono, almost-60, who grew up in San Diego, California. She's a long-time traditional Chinese medicine and qigong practitioner. With her cropped silver hair, white smile and West Coast accent, she sometimes reminds me of an elegant old-style movie star.

Sono's been learning to surf with me for three years. For the last year or so, she's been making the slow, often-awkward transition from the whitewater to the lineup out the back. Her fabulous blue 9-foot Van Straalen longboard is her bridge between beginnerhood and flight across the faces of unbroken green waves. She's pacing herself mindfully for a long surfing life after her late start at 56.

There's Karyn who at 53, is a grandmother, dedicated speech therapist, advocate for children's healthy development, and a fitness fiend. She looks like Jerry Hall with her long legs, blonde hair and smashing eyelashes. She's been learning to surf for just over a year and is, I reckon, the savviest learner-surfer I've taught so far. Her fitness stands her in great stead every session and she's in the midst of ditching her 8-foot softtop foamie for her first fibreglass board.

Then there's Ruthie. She's a tall, strong Murwillumbah music lover who's dreamed of surfing since she was a girl. She's 40-something, works in administration at a local university, and carries a dry sense of humour like a roughed-up backpack wherever she goes. She's been learning to surf for about three years in our dawn sessions and just recently caught every green wave she went for out the back. She reckons she's "a breath away from the other side" where her take offs will connect with her speed and stability on the ride across the faces of waves, and she's right. She's about to put it all together and rip.

Me, I've been at this for years, and for six of them, miraculously, as a surf instructor. I don't look like an old-style Californian movie star or Jerry Hall. I don't even carry my sense of humour around like a backpack.

But since learning to surf at Lennox in my mid-forties, I have the excitement of a teenager, the heart of a poet, an incorrigible devotion to the ocean, and the burning desire to give voice to older women who surf.

We are the generation or more who missed our chance to surf in the 1970s and 1980s when shortboards blazed their way across surfing communities around the world and so many of the guys who rode them, shamelessly chased us out of the water.

With the advent of surf schools and female instructors, and the long-time inspiration of champions like Pam Burridge, Pauline Menczer, Lisa Anderson and Layne Beachley, we are taking our chances a second time around in our mid- and later- life and reclaiming surfing with a vengeance.

Women are out in the water in droves these days.

From tiny, light-as-a-feather little girls to shortboard shredders and the ladies of the longboards stepping delicately from the tail to the nose of their boards, we are at pretty much every surfable beach around the world.

We are a wildly diverse community from all cultures and walks of life and with a myriad of reasons

for paddling out. Some are competing and racking up their wave count. Some are venturing out for their first-ever surf with an intense mix of fear and excitement igniting their hearts. Lots are somewhere in between.

We are here. Now.

When my local righthand point break and the 'office' where I teach surfing feels overrun with eager surfers, I usually take to one of the many beach breaks that run the length of the Gold Coast. And when I do, more often than not I feel like the oldest female surfer out there.

It took a long time to rustle up the courage to paddle out at these breaks and charge the waves that smash onto sand banks with board-and-back-breaking thumps, sending spray shearing backwards in blinding beauty.

But these days I'm out there often, on my retro 7-foot 10-inch, single fin, Surfers Country surfboard that is fast and loose and fun. I call her Zen after my own spiritual practice of sitting meditation and mindfulness guided by Thich Nhat Hahn and my own living teachers.

*Everything I do in my daily life nourishes my longevity in surfing ... I know I will surf until I die.*

I still grapple at times with thoughts of unworthiness while I'm out there in those beach break lineups. I pray I'm not a liability getting in people's way and that my hard-won skills will hold their own in the face of the blokes and young women who mostly shred shortboards and expect other surfers to do the same.

There are lots of older guys out there too – the ones known generically as "old mate" – and sometimes I wonder what an older woman is secretly called... "old maid" perhaps. Or maybe I'm as invisible in the water as I often feel on land?

Nevertheless I am here. Charging, laughing, marvelling, loving this second chance to surf and letting it guide the course of the life I have in me. Everything I do in my daily life nourishes my longevity in surfing including what I eat, how I exercise, how and what I think, and my bedtime hours and sleeping patterns. I know I will surf until I die.

Fittingly, beautifully, karmically, my surfing mentors are men. Some are long-time surfers in their 50s and 60s including Gaz, Dave and Pete, and some are young dudes like my nephew Mackie. I love them for their generous wisdom and endless inspiration.

Bless the women in the water. Especially we oldies like Sono, Karyn, Ruthie and me. We bring a sense of wonder and worship to everything we experience out there because it's taken us so damn long to give it another go.

Like the tide we fell and now we rise. ◎

# Flight

*The gannets are back.*
*On these stormy autumn days*
*overripe with wind and rain*
*and moody grey swells,*
*these early risers ride the sou'easters*
*wearing their new-found, cross-continental feathers –*
*wingtip to wingtip tortoiseshell speckles, which*
*through the cooling season will radiate into*
*pure white and gold.*

*Nothing is separate, this we know.*
*The cloud in the tea cup is*
*the soil, the rain, the sun*
*the plants, the people who pick the leaves and*
*pack the leaves and send them around the world*
*so we can inhale their kindness and*
*taste their sweet healing and give thanks*
*for connection and relationship and warmth.*
*This is ecology.*

*The gannets are back.*
*The early risers with their joyful wings*
*are riding the sou'easters*
*celebrating their new-found, cross-continental flight.*

# Play

The swell is not what I expect today. Across its glassy shades of grey that seep into sky, there are silhouettes and stick figures dotted and clustered along the sandbanks and breaks, but the forecast of a two to three foot nor'easterly swell is being swamped by the Christmas-New Year king tide.

I stand on the sand, watching; then go through the daily yoga motions that help connect me to the energy of the sea. My arms reach to the sky bringing the wisdom of the past and the promise of the future into the perfect present as my hands join in an uplifted prayer position. I inhale.

Hingeing from the hips, knees slightly bent, I fold my torso forward and down. The palms of my hands and soles of my feet soften onto Mother Earth. I exhale.

I extend my right leg back into a deep lunge, then step into the yoga posture known as downward facing dog, breathing slowly as I gaze at the world upside down between my knees. My right leg drives forward, taking my body into another deep lunge before stepping back into 'down dog' again. I hover for a few seconds in a stationary high plank, then do two slow push-ups and arch into upward facing dog, rolling my shoulders down my back and opening my heart up to the sky. It's back into 'down dog' one more time for five slow breaths, lengthening my neck, drawing shoulder blades into my back pockets, breathing energy through my whole body, before I hop my feet towards my hands, folding forward once more then rising to 'high prayer' position, and finally into the stillness of mountain pose, releasing all expectations through my open hands.

All the while, I'm watching the waves, the surfers, the peaks, the rides; touching the wind, leaning into the sea, feeling grounded and energised.

Then I lift my surfboard, tuck it under my right arm and pause to whisper my surfing mindfulness verse: *"Standing on the shore, I feel the earth beneath my feet, beneath the sand. I let the sound of the ocean wash through me. Breathing in, I give thanks for the gift of surfing in my life; breathing out, I paddle out with peace and joy in my heart."*

> "
> We are never more fully alive,
> more completely ourselves,
> or more deeply engrossed in anything,
> than when we are at play.
> "
>
> Charles E Shaefer

This is my pre-surf stretch and mindfulness time. it's an honouring and celebration of Mother Earth, it's a pause in the space between land, sea and sky.

I launch myself and my elegant 8-foot 8-inch timber surfboard "Harriet" through the shorebreak of the central beach and paddle south east through seaward light towards the rock wall. With easy breathing, I pay attention to softening my hands as they catch and pull the water. I notice the muscles moving in my back, finding the strong, strappy latissimus dorsi (or lats) and accessing their leverage and power to smoothly trim the board through saltwater ruffles and bumps.

There's just one other surfer out by the rock wall and he swears he saw waves breaking here as he scoured the surf from the boardwalk earlier. We laugh as approaching sets of waves collapse into deep water holes and disappear.

There's no purchase to be found here so I paddle northwards to a crowd of fibreglass and fins. Still there is no joy or waves, but beyond the red and yellow flags signalling safety for swimmers, I spy some breakers streaming towards the shore. More paddling north – I've now propelled myself perhaps a kilometre without riding a single wave – and there is play to be had at last.

Shorebreak sliders roll towards the beach offering longboarders with good power-to-weight ratios and committed arms, pointlessly playful moments running to the right before slamming into sand. I finally grab this morning with both hands and for two hours, slipstream in and paddle back out in a pattern and pulse of sun-bleached grins.

In the fifteen years since I first learned to surf, the profound, pointless play of riding waves of watery-energy has guided me into career, work and life changes that mean more time to surf and play every day. I escaped the visceral grip of chronic workaholism that had worn me down for over two decades. I grasped the chance to teach others – mainly middle-aged women – about the grace of play through surfing. And I've personally spent thousands of hours unashamedly, in fact brazenly, playing in the ocean with beloved sticks of fibreglass and timber. In the process, I believe play has changed my brain and lifted me out of a tendency towards anxiety and depression.

These days we all know that play is essential for children's development. We know that the ages between zero and eight are a time when children's brains expand perhaps exponentially, with synapses and circuits streaking to connect, particularly during play. At the same time physical, social and emotional growth also blossoms through play.

As the fields of neuroscience and neurobiology flourish, they offer us extraordinary insights into the workings, plasticity, adaptability and flexibility of the brain. Beyond those critical developmental years of zero to eight, we now know that given stimulus, engagement and opportunities to practice, our adult brains will continue to develop. The field of trauma therapy works actively with this knowledge to help adults and children of all ages, defuse traumatic events and triggers, and stimulate life-affirming brain and mind functioning.

*...the pointless play of surfing in one's adulthood offers many of us a wondrous chance to pull our lives back in order and align with creativity, resilience, wholeheartedness, joy and gratitude.*

It seems to me that the pointless play of surfing in one's adulthood offers many of us a wondrous chance to pull our lives back in order and align with creativity, resilience, wholeheartedness, joy and gratitude. It has most certainly done that for me ever since that day I learned to surf at Lennox and I feel its delight almost every day of every week.

Immediately following the bushfire, I survived in a state of shock. Everything felt overwhelming as my brain, mind and body recoiled from people, sounds, lights, touch and even my beloved ocean.

During that time I sat one day on the north side of the rock wall of Currumbin Creek and stared bleakly across the creek mouth to the Alley, the place I had called my (surfing) temple for so many years. It symbolised all the play and joy I had lived inside for so long and now it felt desperately distant. At that moment, it was simply an image of all I felt I had lost.

Soon after that ashen encounter, a long-awaited surf trip with my tribe of surfing friends arrived and I decided to go with them to the beach house we'd rented, if only to have a break from my smoke-and-siren-filled mountain community. I didn't know if I'd cope in a house full of people but I wanted to give it a go.

On our first morning at the beach house, the surf was pumping. I gathered my wits and my beautiful longboard and two of us, Pete and I, headed to the back beach while the rest of the crew hit the point. Pete is one of my dearest friends. To me, he is a tall, fit, superhero surfer and human being of great skill and courage. He's a quiet mentor to me in many ways not least of which is surfing.

When we got to the beach I waved Pete into the water and went through my stretches on the sand, my hands and heart trembling. My mind was a fog of fear, but if not now, when would I ever paddle out again?

I launched myself into the water and began paddling. A brahminy kite circled overhead. Out the back a small line-up of surfers was playing on smooth, glassy sets of head high waves. I paddled towards them. I looked carefully. I felt the water stream through my fingers. And as my body reconnected with the elements, so benign and kind on this clear morning, I began to sob because I could feel joy again, tickling my ribs. I thought to myself *"Surely I am allowed to feel joy again aren't I? Surely, in spite of all the losses and shock and fear and trauma, there is still room in my life to play and laugh? I am allowed that aren't I?"*

And I grabbed that joy with all my heart on that glorious day. I believe my first surf in the aftermath of the fire, signalled to my brain, mind and body that there was still a primary place for play in my life. I recommitted to play as an adult and my determination rose to see this awful time through.

I am so grateful for that surf that day with my buddy Pete. We caught some cracking waves. We laughed and hooted each other and we surfed until our arms ached. It was that day I remembered how to smile again and give myself unconditional permission to play and feel joyfulness no matter how hard the circumstances.

In the long journey of recovery, it was one of my first steps towards crafting a new type of wholeheartedness. I love that the pointless play of surfing has now, twice, delivered deep meaning to my life. ◎

# Tea time

After the groundswell and vigorous beach breaks,
the sweet southerly swell tiptoes toward the point.
Tilting her head and peeking
around the corner,
she decides the coast is clear enough to
set her table for tea,
with a crocheted cloth and lace runners
for longboarders to delicately step upon.
Make no sudden moves or your rails will dig and
your nose will dive;
This is a dance for those with the lightest
of touch and a kindness of spirit.

Below our surfboards, a rocky reef rises as the tide falls.
We glimpse green glints when the sunlight blinks and
screeds of seaweed inhale, exhale, and
expand towards the surface as
we slide on by with wide eyes and shrinking fins.

Dusk draws down and
the offshore cumulus ignite
in a skyward explosion of pink.
The sinking sun and the rising moon
high five,
and before the light shuts off into night
we paddle towards bed and blessed sleep.

*Our job is to embody an*
*undivided heart.*

Susan Murphy

# The glowing world

*"When by the side of the ancient ferry
The breeze and the moonlight are cool and pure,
The dark vessel turns into the glowing word"*

~ Hongzhi

The morning is soft. Winter soft, though it's only autumn. The ocean is rolling, expressing herself in foaming waves that sigh in time with the rising sun. Soft light, breathless, pirouettes around the seasons like silk.

Six weeks ago this ocean was so toxic it was bereft of humanity; not a single surfer or swimmer was to be found in her waters. Queensland and New South Wales were reeling from unmitigated floodwaters that surged through every river and stream, bleeding out into our once-pristine coastlines. Goodness knows what was in there. It stank.

Six weeks ago Russia invaded the Ukraine, tilting Europe towards war yet again and we saw civilian blood running through ancient streets and alleys. We were, still are, powerless to prevent such mayhem and atrocities.

The dark ferry glowered. We scrambled in sorrowful neighbourhoods trying to recover our footing.

Yet here I am now, feet on damp sand, studying the swell with the intent of a sea eagle scanning for the flash of underwater silver. I inhale and exhale deeply, drawing my breath into belly and legs. I stretch my limbs and spiral my joints – shoulders, hips, knees and ankles – testing strength and suppleness. I gather in energy like a wizard or a surf witch, matching my flow to that of the waves and the ocean...here now, here now.

Then, releasing any attachment to outcomes, I lift my beautiful surfboard 'Harriet', tuck her under my arm and with a bow, enter the sea. We paddle together, Harriet and me, stretching out across moving surfaces as we ride the rip and weave through incoming waves to the line-up which is miraculously scattered, quiet and respectful – a rare thing indeed on the Gold Coast.

I take my place, surely the oldest woman out here in this majority of men. I never expect preferential treatment. At 60 years old, I deeply appreciate being 'one of the boys', so to speak. I scan the horizon for approaching lumps that might just wall up into rideable waves as they encounter the sand banks and a sense of the shallows. I feel the lift of the Wild Inside waking up as water rolls beneath the board I sit quietly upon, my hands folded softly in my lap.

And then she comes, a whisper, a lump, a running wall and I pivot in a blink to line myself up with sunlight energy that's travelled from half a world away. Self-talk is clear and concise: *"Keep paddling."* *"Look right."* *"Chest up."*

I go. And in the going I commit body, heart, mind and soul to this moment. I hold onto nothing and hold nothing back as I feel the delicious lift of take-off. I don't remember the spring to my feet.

*As fast as we blink awake and fly, inevitably we must bow and leave this ride; empty handed with a heart full of life.*

I don't remember for even a second how that happened because I am instantly upright and flying, hair on fire across the face of this speeding beast. There is only one-pointed focus on the wave's texture and tilt, with surfboard fins and rails holding in a miracle of physics. In all that speed I touch the still point where a moment is an hour or a lifetime and land life is obliterated. There are just my feet on Harriet, Harriet on this wave, and exhilaration.

As fast as we blink awake and fly, inevitably we must bow and leave this ride; empty handed with a heart full of life. Today in this wave-swept, watery place of exhilarating rides and simple self-talk, where the present – this moment – grabs us by the scruff of our necks, I have touched the glowing world and as Hakuin's *"Song of Zazen"* sings, I have found:

*"Nirvana is right here before our eyes;*
*This very place is the Lotus Land,*
*This very body, the Buddha."*

# Making amends

*Black plastic billows in the breeze,*
*a hungry ghost ravelling string fingers around*
*mangrove twigs and tendrils that reach, beseechingly, across the water.*
*Two weeks ago this creek was a raging torrent*
*sweeping all before it through the suburbs.*
*Today she is serene and so I paddle, watchfully, upon her shine,*
*wary of the jolt of submerged trees or*
*timber limbs grabbing my board and pitching me headlong into mud.*

*There is the grey heron with its guttural call*
*all elegance until it honks across the morning.*
*There is the conference of currawongs*
*convening somewhere in the casuarinas that fringe the banks.*
*Such a concert of calls I wonder what they're on about.*
*Maybe they speak with urgency of Country's pain,*
*adding their voices to the cacophony*
*of drought, fire, flood and white heat that herald*
*things are already on the move to tip the balance for good?*
*Or bad. Or worse.*
*Half a world away Putin tilts Europe towards war and once again*
*we watch aghast, powerless.*
*In the midst of terror, horror, suffering and the rigours of survivor guilt*
*there is still for us - unharmed right now - a chance to cultivate deep intimacy with this place.*

The red beacon on the hill at night is like a campfire calling us home.
The eucalypt forest spreading its fingers through these suburbs,
catches the southerlies and autumn stars in twinkling nights.
We build food forests in the front yard and gratefully harvest the
first baby squash and zucchinis,
homegrown leafy greens filling our lunch boxes and bellies.
And there is the big rainbow bed where we love and laugh and spoon and sleep.

I work in the local supermarket to make ends and beginnings meet.
Each person who comes through receives a smile, a warm greeting, a word of peace,
because this too is place and intimacy and tenderness in action.
Who knows what burdens we each carry
and I resolve to live each moment, person by person, life by life with
deep kindness, mindful of all our losses.

I paddle my board to the beseeching, flood-wrapped mangrove tree.
Carefully I hold her limbs and unravel, shred by shred,
black plastic hungry ghost.
Speaking endearments of release,
we delicately part – plastic, tree, me,
and I ferry the folds of darkness back to shore
gently placing them in the council bin with a bow.
Sunlight skitters downstream.

> *Our job is not to clear up the mystery,*
> *but to make the mystery clear.*
>
> Roshi Robert Aitken

# Spirit

> *We live by the sheer generosity of a moment-to-moment miracle, and it is called the breath. Actually, we could say we live and die by this miracle. Every breath out is a practice of yielding the self to the universe; every breath in is a reincarnation event, the self, reborn, fresh.*

Susan Murphy, Upside Down Zen

# Our breath is the great enabler

I'm out surfing in the lineup at Currumbin Alley on a classic spring morning. Currumbin Rock, our temple, is upstanding in the morning light.

Its tutu of rock shelf gathers in the sou'easterly swell then refracts it north and east towards Palm Beach and Burleigh.

It's a longboard day, which is to say that these aquamarine waves are about thigh high as they meet the Alley's sandbanks and roll through in wide arcs towards the shore. It's perfect conditions for nine-foot plus surfboards ridden by more mellow surfers who like to walk forward and back in a dance of delightful cross-steps between the tail and nose of their boards.

As I wait my turn to claim a wave to for myself, a longboarder, their body stretched along the length of their board, arms and legs moving with extreme intent to grab and pull through the water and paddle into a perfect two-foot roller, passes inches from me. I hear the intentional exhale from their mouth – haaaaaaaaaaa – a nanosecond before they spring cat-like to their feet and hitch a ride on a wondrous, watery wave of sunlight energy.

The sound of their exhale at that moment of energetic connection between human, ocean and joy, stays with me, reverberating through my body and mind; signalling a huge lesson learned about surfing. The breath is an enabler for focused, purposeful, streamlined action.

The conscious use of the breath is a gamechanger in surfing and in life, not only in how we catch and ride waves in the sea and on land, but also in how we manage our anxiety, worry, mindset and self-talk.

We swim in a sea of stress in our lives some days don't you think? From traffic gridlock to supermarket queues, screaming toddlers to high pressure workplaces and sometimes the circumstances of our days seem almost too much to bear.

What if you could access a magic wand to calm everything down? What if you could access that wand 24 hours a day, seven days a week for no cost at all?

Incredibly, you can.

That magic wand is called the breath. It is undeniably available to us 24/7, otherwise we'd be dead. But most of us don't consciously think of it or remember to use its power. Most of us race around like mice, sipping bits of air that sit high in our chests and with our shoulders locked up somewhere near our ears.

In this chaotic, crazy-busy world, most of us don't know the multitude of ways the breath can save us from stress-overload. Let's have a little look at the ways and means...these include practices including meditation, yoga, qigong, breathing exercises and nose breathing.

For much of my life I was a study in perpetual motion, physically and mentally. My system (body, mind, brain and nervous system in particular), had adapted by always being vigilant and busy. I was always planning projects, doing stuff, and literally running everywhere because that was the only way I subconsciously knew how to block out the chaos I'd experienced early on.

I didn't know any other way until just before my 50th birthday when a dear friend taught me a form of breathing called Japa as well as a type of sitting meditation that my system enjoyed. Japa is an ancient Indian practice that links deep, slow breathing with an affirmation or mantra. I chose "So Hum" which means "I am that" – a part of all life.

To practice Japa, on my deep, slow inbreath through my nose, I would say to myself "So", and on my long outbreath I would internally say "Hum". The aim is to practice this deep breathing and mantra repetition continually – driving the car, shopping, working, surfing, eating and so on. Of course I fell out of it often, but I improved at noticing when my attention had drifted and then, without judgement, I'd simply return to my breath and my mantra.

Within about two weeks I noticed that something very interesting was going on in my brain, in my mind and also in my nervous system. I was slowing down. I was feeling calmer. I was starting to do one thing at a time instead of constantly multi-tasking. I realised that if I continued with this practice of Japa, everything could change...my brain, mind, heart, nervous system and perhaps even how I lived my life. I decided it was time to make a choice – to return to my old manic ways or continue to do Japa and see what happened.

I chose Japa, and over weeks, months and years the practice has trained my mind-body system to become steadier, calmer, more composed, equanimous and awake. It's felt like a miracle to be honest. That monkey-mind of mine, which was always planning, preparing, organising, worrying, grieving, regretting, wondering and so on, responded to breath and mind training like a dog or horse. Instead of running me ragged, I found a disciplined ally and companion within myself.

At the same time as learning and practising Japa, my dear friend also taught me a form of sitting meditation that was actively challenging enough for me to try. I learned how to sit still for 30 minutes every day and I learned to look forward to and love this dedicated time of stillness and deep, slow breathing.

As I practised, I felt enormous energy begin to flow through my body and mind. When I engaged with the world I felt more in tune and aligned.

Japa and meditation changed my life at the age of 50 and I continue to practice them devotedly every day. I access their power and discipline solely through my breath and everything else flows from that. I return to the feel of the breath against my nostrils as I inhale, and as I exhale, I imagine old stale energy moving out of my body. In and out, in and out 24/7.

This awareness of the power of my breath also transformed my long-time yoga practice. I was able to teach myself to rest in the breath, even in the most uncomfortable yoga postures in difficult yoga classes.

As yoga practitioners, we know that the word yoga means "to yoke" – it refers to the breath yoking or connecting the body and the mind throughout our practice. All we need to do is keep the breath mindfully flowing deeply through our body, and our minds will experience feelings of steadiness and calmness, ease and flow.

The more we practice this deep breathing, the more calmness, ease and flow we will feel, even in the hardest of times.

The ancient Chinese mindful movement practices of qigong and tai chi work in very similar ways, using the inhalation to fill and nourish the body with energy and lifeforce (qi); while the outbreath expels old, stale, unhelpful energy. At the same time, our body moves through a series of stretches and flows that support the integration of the mind and body.

One of the most powerful books yet to be written about the breath is by journalist James Nestor and is simply called *"Breath"*. This wonderful journey through the world of conscious breathing has two central messages for us: the power of nose breathing and the power of long, slow, deep breathing.

James Nestor says, *"...there's a foundation of habitual breathing we can all use and build upon regardless of whether you're an asthmatic, and ultra-marathoner, or prone to anxiety.*

*"First, breathe through your nose and breathe through your nose all the time. Second, breathe slowly. This doesn't mean to make breathing a hassle or to force it, it should be light. It should be slow and it should be deep...You get more oxygen by breathing less, by breathing slowly"* (James Nestor in The Sunday Magazine, CBC Radio, July 25 2021).

Nose breathing offers these benefits:

- Reduces exposure to foreign substances
- Humidifies and warms inhaled air
- Increases air flow to arteries, veins and nerves
- Increases oxygen uptake and circulation
- Slows down breathing
- Improves lung volume
- Helps the diaphragm to work properly
- Lowers the risk of allergies and hay fever
- Reduces the risk of coughing
- Aids the immune system
- Lowers the risk of snoring and sleep apnea
- Supports the correct formation of teeth and mouth.

Taking long, deep breaths helps us to voluntarily regulate our autonomic nervous system which can have many benefits including:

- Lowering the heart rate
- Regulating blood pressure
- Helping relaxation
- Decreasing the release of the stress hormone cortisol
- Relieving pain
- Stimulating the lymphatic system (which can help detoxify the body)
- Improved immunity
- Increased energy
- Improved digestion

Internationally respected qigong master teacher Lee Holden, also has important things to say about the breath. As a qigong teacher and practitioner of over 30 years standing, it's fair to say that he, more than most, lives by conscious breathing.

About the breath and calming the nervous system he says:

*"When you breathe with an awareness of your breath, your attention naturally flows into your body and your mind relaxes. It stops searching for external threats which is why conscious breathing is the fastest way to calm your mind (and reduce anxiety while at the same time increasing your energy).*

*"So whenever you feel anxious...whenever your mind is spinning...whenever you want to get back into your body, just pause. Close your eyes if you can. Centre. Empty all the air out of your lungs and take three full, deep breaths.*

*"Start your breath in the lower abdomen and let it rise through your body like a wave. Let your breath completely fill you up...then breathe out from the top of your lungs down to your abdomen.*

*"Breathe and watch as your mind calms down. Breathe and watch as your body relaxes. Breathe and watch as you re-centre."* (Lee Holden Qigong, holdenqigong.com)

The power of nose breathing.
The power of the inhale.
The power of the exhale.
The power of slow breathing.
The power of deep breathing.

Our Breath is the Great Enabler. ◎

# The encounter

*Adrift.*
*Burnt orange and black spread-eagled across*
*the languid river –*
*liquid reflecting big sky and mountains.*
*I kneel and sweep these sweet wings*
*as fine as tissue*
*into my cupped hands and*
*suddenly there is life arising!*
*The fluttering is a heartbeat of hope as*
*this beauty alights like an intake of breath upon*
*the prow of my paddleboard.*

*A monarch,*
*on tiptoes she lights up this day*
*as sunshine across water,*
*pure energy vibrating towards Wollumbin, the Cloud Gatherer mountain*
*and as I drift downstream,*
*zephyrs of air feather my spirit.*

*Before I make landfall beside the bridge*
*I nudge us into a crowd of lilies cramming the riverbank.*
*If this butterfly needs to rest or die,*
*better it be within the green of the Great Earth*
*where her colours can merge with roots and dirt.*
*We slide gently in, together she and I.*
*My quiet fingers extend and she steps*
*as delicately as a kiss, upon the index*
*then, confidently she is gone in a flicker of uplift so sweet that I swoon.*
*Life and my heart are carried onwards in the breeze.*

# Poetry in motion

The morning air is cool and soft. A cornflower blue sky
arcs overhead with no sign of where it begins or ends.

Our feet, some bare upon the grass, some clad in comfortable shoes, seek the feel of the earth beneath our soles. The small lake outside the community centre where we gather, is dotted with lily pads and awakening flowers. It is as still and silent as a mirror.

We feel the breath move across our nostrils as we inhale and we consciously draw it down through our chests, ribs and diaphragm, noticing expansion in our bellies like an air-filled balloon. As we exhale, we imagine the breath travelling in a ribbon of golden light up our spines until it spirals around the inside of our skulls. On the next inhale we draw the air-light back down into our bellies, mindfully circling breath and energy through our bodies in a cycle known as the 'microcosmic orbit'.

Here on this beautiful day beside the lake, a group of about 20 of us – of mixed ages, genders, and states of health and fitness – is practising a form of ancient Chinese exercise and meditation known as qigong (pronounced chee-gong). "Qi" for lifeforce energy and "gong" meaning skilled practice.

We have become something of a quiet tribe over the years, sharing our breath and slices of our lives each Monday morning when we soften the public facades between us beneath big skies. Inside our tribe are avid bird watchers and readers of books, women living through and recovering from breast cancer, people living with disabilities and their carers, bushwalkers, retirees, people suffering from anxiety, depression and grief, full-time, part-time and casual workers managing their work-life balance and stress levels, grandparents, parents and so many more.

As we each cross the threshold of the community centre to step onto the grass by the lake, or in hot seasons, into the air-conditioned green room, we seem to release the rushing that got us here and relax into each other's warm company to breathe and move energy through our bodies, exhaling the stress and tension of busy days and perhaps traumatic times. Together we stretch, activate energy and move in meditative flows which fill us with feelings of peace, calm and centredness at the beginning of each working week.

For optimal health, we need body and spirit, exercise and meditation, awareness of the inner world and the outer. In other words, health requires balance and moderation. The goal of qigong may be summarised as xing ming shuang xui, spirit and body equally refined and cultivated. Cultivate your whole being, as you would cultivate a garden with attention, care and even love.

Ken Cohen

In truth, I don't remember my first experience of qigong, but somehow I knew it existed separately to the complex sequences of tai chi that I've never been able to remember or flow serenely with. When a request was made many years ago for a tai chi/qigong class at the local community centre where I already taught fitness and yoga classes, I felt capable enough to offer a hybrid mindful movement experience. Thus began an intimate and ongoing love affair with the rhythms and flow of this practice, with me finding and learning online qigong moves at home and bringing them to a slowly-growing group of patient locals.

This ancient slow-motion martial art also seductively offered a deepening of peace for my own monkey mind which had driven me into a state of perpetual motion for decades.

I began my crash course in online qigong by propping my phone on the railing of the front verandah of the 'Storybook Cottage' in the mountains and connecting to a few Eastern and Western teachers whose styles seemed to match my temperament and constitution.

Cue sunrise with shafts of ethereal light climbing through clouds to breathe warmth across my yawning wintertime verandah. Loaded up with jumpers and scarves I'd *'knock on the door of life'*, rotating side-to-side from hips and waist, swinging my arms

to lightly slap lower back and belly, then knock on my chest and then clap upper shoulders with open palms. All the while breathing steam in the crisp mountain air. At times I'd struggle to remember the poetry of names like *'painting with light'* or *'grasping pharaoh's tail'*. Sometimes I'd be left reeling with their fluid beauty, and race to grab pen and paper to make notes that would guide my teaching.

As weeks stretched into months and then into years, these regular sessions seemed to nourish my nervous system. Deep rhythmic patterns of breathing that matched the flows of movement seemed to settle my system in ways that hugged my 30-year-long yoga practice and took it free diving into places where peace and stillness reside. The joys of feeling steady, awake and present – all at the same time – were and still are compelling.

*Deep rhythmic patterns of breathing that matched the flows of movement seemed to settle my system...*

Even my surfing inexplicably improved as my qigong practice deepened. I don't really know how or why, but my capacity to align my own energy with that of the ocean before paddling out into the surf, seemed to grow, and more often than not I could meet the ocean without expectations and dance with its big patterns and energies.

In March 2020, when COVID reached Australia's shores, extending its frightening tentacles into every home and community, we all went into lockdown. My community centre classes ceased and, like so many millions of people, my income flatlined.

In collaboration with the community centre, I raced to create an online platform for my classes. I realised more than ever before, how vital movement, exercise, mindfulness and social connection are to all of us. Without any guarantee of payment, I began hosting my classes, including qigong, from home; reaching out through online technology to connect with my community tribe. It kept me feeling useful and I hope it kept many people in touch.

When the federal government's early superannuation access scheme was opened in mid-2020, in response to COVID-related job and economic losses, I saw a long-awaited dream come to life. I leaped at the chance to enrol in formal, online qigong teacher training with Lee Holden's school in Santa Cruz, on the other side of the world.

Without a second thought I jumped in, bare-feet and all, and through the guts of COVID, for more than six months, I studied, trained, learned, practised and read, astounded at the depth and breadth of this form of 'exercise'.

In the process, I needed to ditch most of my previous informal online learnings and begin again; systematically dismantling my cobbled-together technique and rebuilding my practice from the ground up. I felt humbled in every way and was grateful to undertake these formal studies.

My brain worked overtime to remember new and exciting concepts and movements and it was a blessing to apply myself deeply to studying again.

The benefits of online technology too! How astounding to access international expertise any time of the day or night and then translate that immediately into my own YouTube and Zoom classes for my community classes on the Gold Coast and beyond.

I graduated successfully as a Level 1 Holden Qigong teacher in late 2020. When COVID lockdowns ceased, my in-person classes started up again at the community centre and they continue to this day.

The Monday morning tribe still meets by the beautiful lake or indoors, and for about an hour we base ourselves entirely inside our bodies and our breath.

There is nowhere else for us to go, there is nowhere else for us to be. For a miraculous stretch of time we have all the time we need and peace prevails within us all as we quietly stretch, energise and flow together like poetry in motion. ◎

# Etchings

Two seconds more light today.
Once again the Winter Solstice has moved through us
in the dark
and, surviving, we ignite fires inside and out and
give thanks for what has been.
With love we release what was tight.
With intent, we paddle into a rising swell
and turn metallic grey ocean swept by south winds
into soft sunrises over low-tide beaches
where terns gather in salt-water reflections.

On the mountain where my shoulders steel themselves
against descending cold,
we congregate under the naked red cedar,
lying on her dry leaves that have fallen
one by lovely one over autumn
and gaze longingly through bare branches to the sky.
A frenzy of finches with their whirring winglets and
yellow breasts
explodes into our silence
and we wake astonished
turning our hearts toward spring and hope and warmth.

In the old bathtub out the back
the micro kitchen-garden grows.
Those fragile seedlings I nestled into potting mix
six weeks ago,
are strong.
New-life lettuce, kale, English spinach and coriander
hear the call of the marigolds
and rise
offering expansive leaves in delicious green bouquets.
As the magpies and butcher birds astound us with
their operatic mastery –
spiralling birdsong through the creases of
the neighbourhood –
I sit still
I set sail
and give myself over to life.

" 

*Because you are alive,*
*everything is possible.*

"

Thich Nhat Hanh

# Practising Zen

Have you noticed the way the word "Zen"
captures the imagination? It seems Zen
is everywhere – in zen landscaping, zen
furniture, zen highrises, zen holidays and
luxurious zen retreat centres, to name but
a few. It's like everyone wants a bit of zen.

In fact, zen simply means to sit
in meditation.

Australian Zen teacher Susan Murphy suggests there are many misconceptions about Zen. She says,

*"In popular culture it has come to mean something like a cool detachment from everyday life. But that misses the point entirely. Zen is vital, engaged, passionate and active. It celebrates the mystery of being here in our mysterious bodies. When we sit in meditation and experience ourselves completely, we discover that we are not separate from the universe, but a complete part of its miraculous unfolding."* (Zen Open Circle, zenopencircle.org.au)

I have been a long-time admirer of the Vietnamese Zen monk and teacher Thich Nhat Hanh, who is revered for his peaceful, unconditionally loving energy and wise teachings. Like many others around the world, I also deeply respect his ability to synchronise devoted spiritual practice with masterful social and environmental activism. Indeed, Martin Luther King (MLK) in 1967, nominated Thay (as he's fondly known by his students – which is Vietnamese for 'teacher'), for the Nobel Peace Prize for his engaged activism during the Vietnam war. Thay also deeply influenced MLK's work, particularly around the idea of the 'sangha' or community of spiritual practice which was integral to Thay's tradition of Zen. Martin Luther King adapted the notion of the sangha into that of the 'beloved community', where every human being was welcomed and belonged.

In 1966 Thay was exiled from Vietnam after expressing opposition to the Vietnam war and refusing to take sides. In 1982 he and his students found land in south west France and established the Plum Village mindfulness practice centre and monastery. It was here he lived and taught until 2018 when he returned to Vietnam and peacefully passed away on January 22, 2022 aged 95 years old.

The practice of Zen (yes, it's a practice which means we show up every day to sit in meditation), traces its origins to India but it was formalised in China during the Tang dynasty. Chan, as Zen is known in China, was transmitted to Japan and took root there in the thirteenth century. It also spread south to Vietnam and northeast to Korea. DT Suzuki (1870-1966), a Japanese Buddhist scholar and thinker, wrote numerous essays and books in English to introduce Zen ideals to Western audiences in the late nineteenth century.

I never imagined practising or becoming a student of Zen, but Zen chose me in about 2017 at a one-day silent retreat on the Gold Coast. I began studying with a beautiful yoga and Zen teacher at my local yoga centre and simply focused on practising sitting meditation every morning for about 20 minutes. I'd sit on my cushion at home to breathe in and out and notice how my mind both wandered and steadied, wandered and steadied.

Two years later, following the bushfire, I experienced deep feelings of anger, despair and a hollowness of spirit, particularly about the onset of climate crisis. I'd devoted so much of my mid-life to educating and communicating the perils of climate destabilisation and advocating for preventative actions at systemic, personal, household and community levels, that the Beechmont fire, followed by the 2020 Black Summer of wildfire seemed to signal all this work was worthless.

I felt the worst fears of environmental activists and climate scientists were coming to pass in this lifetime and I had no idea what to do with that bleak knowledge.

Zen, as I was practising it back in the bushfire time, no longer seemed to have guidance or comfort for me.

In the midst of the bushfire fallout, I met Susan Murphy through her extraordinary book *"Minding the Earth, Mending the World: Zen and the Art of Planetary Crisis"*. In all my despair and feelings of hollowness, Susan's book nourished my spirit with her uniquely Australian, landscape and activist-based approach to Zen, which was so different to any other practices I had encountered. I felt she understood my deep connection to the mountains and oceans where I lived and could hear my grief about the bushfires. I immediately sought out her sangha – her community of spiritual practice – called Zen Open Circle (ZOC) in southern New South Wales. It was a revelation.

For many years ZOC has hosted not only in-person retreats and gatherings, but also reached out across this vast continent and even the world through online technology. As COVID lockdowns descended in March/April 2020, I leaped into ZOC's regular online gatherings and relaxed into the warmth, laughter and openness of this remarkable sangha.

One of my first experiences with ZOC was a study program focusing on the astounding work of Aboriginal man Tyson Yunkaporta in the book *"Sand Talk: How indigenous thinking can save the world"*. Over many months some thirty ZOC practitioners and guests read *Sand Talk*, then shared our feelings and insights in terms of the interweaving of Aboriginal wisdom patterns and Zen practice. In all my years of environmental education and activism, I had never experienced such a rich, fertile, respectful, deep-running conversation, led brilliantly by Susan and her assistant Kynan. I had found my tribe and my spiritual and intellectual home.

It is the warmth, inclusiveness and delight within ZOC that I love. Everyone is invited to share their experiences, thoughts, ideas, poetry and artwork.

Everyone is invited, indeed encouraged, to bring our love of place – this place, this land – to the table and exchange ideas about how, as Zen practitioners, we might help protect and restore this ancient continent, inhabited not only by 230 year's-worth of immigrants, but millennia of First Nations people indigenous to this land; who have tended, managed, stewarded, sung, loved and honoured this land sustainably.

Thich Nhat Hanh's concept of Interbeing – the inseparability of everything – is at the heart of ZOC's approach to Zen and is for me, the doorway that connects Zen practice to daily life.

Thay invites us to notice the cloud in the tea cup as we drink our morning cuppa. By this, he is referring to the clouds and rain that watered the tea bushes, that were growing in the soil and nourished by the sun. He is referring to the farmers who tended, harvested and packed the tea into boxes and shipped them around the world to be reinvigorated and steeped by boiling water in our tea cups first thing in the morning.

Everything is connected. The web of life is intricate, robust, wide and deep. Nothing is separate, not even humans.

Zen teaches us to notice, respect, nourish and tend to these interconnections running through all life on Earth. To take nothing for granted and to marvel at this wondrous mystery. To step up and stand our ground when the health of these systems, cycles and connections are at risk, as they are now. Not in anger or despair; but through our daily practice of sitting with composure, clarity and compassion born from connecting the material, physical world and the present moment with a sense of eternity.

It is here that compassion takes centre stage. Not just as a worthy idea but as a way of acting in and upon the world.

Did you know that humans are the only species of life on Earth with an awareness beyond our own day-to-day survival?

Just think about that for a moment. We are the only species with this extraordinary capacity. We can think *into* the future. We can think *about* the future. We can think about other species and the interconnections between us all. We can think about an entire planet. We are able to recognise that we are just one species of the innumerable species alive at this very moment.

And we can take action beyond securing our own day-to-day and longer-term survival. We can plan and contribute to a future where all species of life on this planet not only survive but thrive. We can do this at micro, personal levels and we can do this at system-scale levels.

That, is muscular compassion. That is compassion in action don't you think? That is an astonishing gift we have and if we don't take muscular, compassionate action now for all life on Earth, when will we?

My practice of Zen and the beautiful work of ZOC and sanghas all around the world, give me hope that we do all, have a future to create and craft together with all life. ◎

# Home in a time of plague

My mother's pyjamas hang loosely on the washing line.
From the kitchen window, speckled with webs,
I watch them – hanging, inanimate,
as the sun reaches from the east across a quiet sky
to light up new leaves on the red cedar.

Today I will walk without the dog, into subtropical bush.
Like a whisper of invisible breeze I will drift past
those busy roadworks that deliver
engineered restraints across this mountain
after wildfire scorched us all.
It's calling me again, that forest.
Any chink in the manmade armour and I'm in;
asking permission to enter only from the Old Ones
and the sea of green
and answered by the keen of black cockatoos and shy butterflies.

In this time of plague and serious news
I pay attention to the way the ground rises to meet my feet;
how the earth and my soles, connect step-by-step.
This is no monologue
it's a dance, it's a song, it's a deep-time songline
and I pray that simple walking
will mind this life.

This home on top of the hill anchors me here.
Nothing is straight or orderly but the way
sunset glows through the kitchen to
ignite every facet in my grandmother's cut-glass bowl
is an afternoon aria.
After almost a year, we are all home again in this study
of light and shade,
pyjamas and forest,
black cockatoos and rising earth.
Nothing is straight or orderly but
at sunrise and sunset we sing.

> *May we turn inwards and stumble upon our true roots in the intertwining biology of this exquisite planet. May nourishment and power pulse through these roots, and fierce determination to continue the billion-year dance.*

John Seed

# Mending the mind, minding the Earth

Think of a place in nature that you love the most. Take your time.
Get comfortable in your chair or lounge or bed or wherever you're reading this.

Notice your breath passing across your nostrils as you breathe in and let your belly fill and expand. As you breathe out, let all tension flow out of your body including your shoulders, neck, head, belly, arms, legs, hands and feet. Let everything soften.

Let's breathe deeply again a few more times: inhaling slowly, then pausing for a few heartbeats; releasing a long exhale, and pausing for a few heartbeats.

Now let your mind picture your favourite place in nature. It might be a beautiful garden or a grassy park you love lying in, in the middle of a busy city. It might be beside a river or a wild beach; it might be a night sky filled with stars on a camping trip; or an exotic forest or waterfall you discovered on an overseas trip. Maybe it's mountains covered with snow?

Let your mind rest in that beloved place: see all its beauty, hear the sounds of birds or breeze or bees, smell its unique fragrances and feel its nourishment, its peace, its gifts of inspiration and happiness. Fill yourself up. Feel the deep and abiding connection you have with that place – an unbreakable bond. Rest in its peace, knowing you can visit there any time in your mind to receive its blessings.

Breathe deeply again...and again...letting yourself feel it all.

When you're ready, gently and slowly begin to return to your body. Wiggle your fingers and toes. Feel the air upon your skin and your body resting wherever you are. Quietly return to this moment, here-now. Have a long stretch right through the arms to the fingertips, right up over your head, then all the way down the legs, feet and toes. Stretch, lengthen, inhale, exhale, relax.

Notice how you're feeling now. Let your awareness travel slowly from the top of your head all the way through each part of your body – into muscles, bones, joints, organs, skin – and take note, without judgement, of what's going on for you physically. Notice too how your thoughts feel. Have they slowed down a little? Are you smiling a bit on the inside?

What a wondrous thing the mind is. To vividly call up every feeling, sight, sound and smell associated with your most special place in nature is extraordinary don't you think? Your mind transported you there didn't it! You felt it in every fibre of your being. You 'mind-surfed' your way there, even if your special place is on the other side of the world or a memory from decades ago.

Here's a secret...

The brain and the mind don't know the difference between what we directly experience and what we imagine. Read that again: The brain and the mind don't know the difference between what we directly experience and what we imagine.

Imagine then, if we could harness the power of our mind and consistently feed our body with nourishment, healing, peace, uplifting and vibrant energy, kindness and compassion? Imagine what that might do to our feelings, thoughts, our health, the structure of our brain (which as we know is plastic and able to physically change at any age), and how we show up in the world?

Did you know you can do this? Did you know you can practice this type of mental exercise every single moment of every single day, and each time you do it, you strengthen and harness the power of your mind in a positive feedback loop?

*Imagine... if we could harness the power of our mind and consistently feed our body with nourishment, healing, peace, uplifting and vibrant energy, kindness and compassion?*

If you were to do this every day for six weeks, it would start to become a healthy mental habit; it would begin to change the physical structure of your brain; it would start to change the way you feel and the type of energy you bring to your life.

It's a simple process and its success simply requires you to do it every day – perhaps a few times a day.

It's a form of meditation and mindfulness, of mental hygiene that trains your mind to focus its attention on one thing at a time; and through your breath and awareness, to feel the grace and nourishment of your most special place in nature.

Are you up for it? Six weeks of daily focus on your special place to see what happens to your mind, energy, brain and body? To see if the peace, calmness, uplift and gratitude associated with that place begins to flow more consistently into your nervous system?

There's the invitation.

And I'm wondering, now that you've revisited that place of beauty and refreshment in your mind and recognised your love and appreciation for all that it gives you, whether you could feel moved to look out for your special place in return? For example, to pick up rubbish that's been dropped there? To teach others about its glorious features and how to protect it? Perhaps even to take action if it is threatened by thoughtless, destructive development? If it were damaged by flood, fire or human impacts, could you feel moved to go there and help restore and regenerate it? To plant trees, remove debris or invasive weeds, to help clean it up and love it up again? Could you consider ways to nourish your special place in return for all it offers to you?

I'm doing something very deliberate and intentional with you here. I'm wanting to:

- Show you how to start harnessing the wild horses in your mind through the mental exercise of recalling in vivid detail your most treasured place in nature while you breathe deeply and fully;

- Invite you to do this as a daily practice that helps to calm, soothe, nourish and uplift your mind-heart-body complex and notice what happens to your system during six weeks as you make this journey in your mind and in the most compelling way, start to practice mindfulness and meditation;

- Help you build a bridge between the power of your mind and the power of love you have for a place, with the potential to take hands-on action to protect, restore or regenerate that place based on your emotional connection and the recognition of the gifts that place gives to you.

That place lives brightly inside your heart and mind, right? It's part of the fabric of your life and who you believe you are, right? It feels like home to go there in person *and* in your mind, right? You love it so much you would help protect it or grieve for it if it was destroyed, right?

Using the same mind-surfing power, do you think you can now picture Earth from space? To imagine that small, blue, jewel-like planet floating in a sea of darkness, just like the photographs we've all seen taken by astronauts and space shuttles.

Take a moment to stand in your special place in nature, hearing, seeing, smelling, feeling all its wonders and then slowly, slowly, slowly pan back from there – through the neighbourhoods and landscapes around your special place; then out further to take in the surrounding towns, villages, counties; then beyond to the surrounding states and countries; then all the way back to see the whole earth in close up; and then way back to see that blue jewel – our home – floating in deep space like a fragile bubble.

This is our home. It is the only planet we know of in the cosmos that supports life in such wondrous abundance that we can all have our own 'special place in nature' and our rich lives.

From your galaxy-wide perspective of Earth, can you see the seasons turning? Can you see the oceans unfurling? Can you see the vast forests and icecaps at the poles? The infinite sky? Can you see the villages, cities and towns filled with people, homes and families; communities, shops, skyscrapers, parks and rivers winding through – some in daylight and some at night with great sheaths of lights spreadeagled across the land? Can you see the butterflies, bees, birds, mammals and reptiles – big cats, elephants, snakes, beetles, worms under the soil? Can you see family farms and the immense industrial-scale agriculture? Wind farms, coal-fired power plants, the people who keep them going and the activities they energise? Can you see wildfires and great floods? Coral reefs and the Amazon rainforest? Look at it all with curiosity, as if you're a visitor from space. No opinions or judgements, just great curiosity.

Look at that wondrous blue jewel of a planet humming and buzzing with life – really truly see it. Now feel it. All that energy, creativity, movement, stillness, delight, despair, wealth, poverty, all those connections. Can you see from this perspective how everything on this wondrous planet is connected? The smallest pollinator to the biggest city? And all protected by a veil of atmosphere to keep us warm enough for life, but not yet too warm for life.

When we harness the wild horses in our minds to focus on both our most beloved place in nature AND on this beloved blue planet hurtling through the immensity of space, we understand that we have the capacity to notice both the small and the huge. We have the capacity to take notice too, of what's going on out there including the cycles and systems that keep all alive AND the fraying and ripping of the fabric of life on Earth: the water, air and soil cycles; the flow of sunlight energy; biodiversity; atmospheric health. All of these (and so many more) that keep us alive are also breaking down and falling apart before our very eyes.

If we harness and focus our minds in this way, if we dare to look deeply at our world, we can also find the capacity to feel compassion and grief for it all. We can find the strength and fortitude to let those feelings rise up and in the rising up, allow them to move us into ways of making hands-on change – taking personal action as well as helping with systemic overhaul – to leave a legacy of life, so that all life can continue to be sustained and this exquisite blue planet restored to health.

Two things at once: personal action and systemic overhaul and they both require focus, determination, vision, commitment, courage, compassion, forgiveness and creativity. Muscular commitment and compassion. Vigorous kindness and determination.

We all know about the personal changes required from us:

- Consume less: power, food, clothing, stuff, water, cars, travel...

- Simplify: homes, transport, workplaces, lives...

- Grow more: food, connectivity, focus, compassion, community, friendship, consciousness.

What about systemic change? When we speak of 'systemic' we're talking about economic, political, educational, health and other systems that overarch our society and civilization. I think many of us know now that capitalism ruled by corporate greed and government blinkeredness must be transformed into systems based on equity, fairness, wellness, inclusion, kindness, compassion, and community with a deep awareness of the connections between all life forms on earth.

This transformation may seem like an impossible task – yet these are systems that have been created by human beings, and therefore they can be dismantled and new systems created by human beings.

We have many examples of this occurring:

- The end of the American slave economy in 1865

- The fall of the Berlin wall in 1989

- The dismantling of apartheid and the creation of democracy in South Africa heralded by the first democratic general election in 1994.

These extraordinary systemic transformations were brought about by many factors including the engagement of everyday people taking action.

Let's play 'what if' for a moment...

*What if, here and now, the best of neuroscience, quantum physics and human consciousness tell us that we are midwiving a new epoch of consciousness in human civilization?*

What if we know enough about the workings of the brain and the mind – through neuroscience, neuroplasticity and contemplative traditions – to recognise that humanity has the capacity to end wars and destructive industrialisation and transform how we live here on Earth?

What if, here and now, the best of neuroscience, quantum physics and human consciousness tell us that we are midwiving a new epoch of consciousness in human civilization? What if we could oversee the death of the old epoch of wars, famine, destruction, power over and separation, with deep and wide wisdom and at the same time, usher in a new age?

What would you do?
How would you choose to show up in such a time? Would you choose to contribute or would you close your eyes and turn away? ◎

# Ecological stronghold

Driftwood emerges from low tide sand,
not drowning, waving
with intricate insect carvings and lettering.
Decorated with a design so elegant
I wonder how Nature could be so effusive
with her windswept beauty
if survival of the fittest still rules?

At our campsite
a blossoming tree is brushed by the collective
wings of butterflies.
They dip, sip, sup
in and out of flowers,
dancing all day and drifting upon breezes
that swing
west to south
setting petals free.

In the mountains –
now luminous after a summer of rain
the vulnerable, venerable Antarctic beech trees
and Albert Lyrebird
regain a foothold upon the earth
in a rare show of seasonal temperance that is
cool and wet.
Our rainforest world rises to meet this sweetness
with open arms
and for a moment,
in this world of extreme heat –
all is well.

Inside coastal sunrises
I paddle into swells where
baby blue mullet tickle my toes and
stingrays sometimes fly through air
to land with a joyful splash of spray.
As we enter autumn
I too begin to find my feet meeting the exhale of earth.
Steady, steady as she goes
inner and outer ecologies re-grow.
I bend to trace the driftwood lace with
tender tips of fingers.
A butterfly dances out to sea.
Antarctic beech trees stretch into sky and sigh.

> *Awaken your spirit to adventure;*
> *hold nothing back, learn to find ease in risk;*
> *soon you will home in a new rhythm,*
> *for your soul senses the world that awaits you.*

John O'Donohue

# The end becomes the beginning

Deep violet light fills the window and the sky.

The forest climbing the hill just beyond our neighbourhood rooftops on the Gold Coast is silent this pre-dawn morning and the red beacon at its summit glows. That beacon perched above the treetops feels like a tribal campfire here in the suburbs as it burns through the night, keeping us safe as we sleep.

I've lived in this neighbourhood tucked between forest and winding Tallebudgera Creek, for well over a year. In late afternoons I walk the hobo dog through local streets, touching the papery bark and supple leaves of local melaleucas, smiling at neighbours who introduce themselves via their dogs.

My favourite walk is to the footbridge that spans the creek – connecting local households to magical Schuster Park where koalas, powerful owls and sacred kingfishers can still be sighted. Sunset light shimmers and glows across the water and for a few minutes most evenings, the sounds of the suburbs fall away as the creek speaks in reflections and tidal flows.

I have a home again thanks to my beloved wife Jen and we live in this place of deep violet dawns and golden afternoon skies with love, laughter and wondrous affection. We tend to the garden of our love consciously and continually, never ever taking what we have for granted. I feel the safest and happiest I have ever felt in my life, here in the arms of Jen.

The hardest part of these past few years was leaving the landscapes of Beechmont and Binna Burra behind. That rainforest. Big Sky. Those cliffs and basalt ramparts glowering below the plateau. The rolling green hills and summertime storms. The creeks and rivers that rise hidden, amongst trees and ancient ferns.

The birds, my god, the birds up there. I once saw a rare Pacific Baza fly at eye height right beside the length of my verandah as I stood rooted to the spot: yellow eye locked into my blue eyes, as the electricity exploded between us.

Cheeky bower birds collecting all things blue. The mewling, sure-footed cat birds. The squadrons of screeching rainbow lorikeets buzzing the Storybook Cottage, the crimson rosellas decked out in their glamorous pantaloons, the king parrots hanging hilariously upside down from roof gutters and peering into widows. The furry, soft eyed marsupials too, who would bless our backyards with their quiet company.

I held tightly to it all for a long time, worried my heart would permanently break if I let it go.

But as the sun and rain and wind and swells swept across the lowlands of the southern Gold Coast this past summer, I've realised my home is here now. It's time not only to love these glorious beaches, but to take these creeks – Tallebudgera and Currumbin – and their muddy, marshy ecosystems deep into my heart. To consciously embed myself in the landscapes of this place and gently, over time, allow the magic of here to seep into my bones.

I am learning its birds by heart and inviting the mud and mangroves to wrap themselves around me. I have joined the local creek-care group and I'm about to start attending their monthly gatherings to help clean up and revegetate the creek's banks.

There's something astounding about experiencing extreme vulnerability; of having everything you cherish ripped apart by catastrophic forces you have no control over.

The bushfire left me reeling emotionally, mentally, physically and spiritually. I felt burned up in every way. I sought help when I realised my usual life-supports were not keeping me afloat, let alone getting me back on my feet again in daily life.

Then COVID hit and the whole world went into lockdown. There was terrible hardship and suffering and we may never be able to calculate the human costs of that time. Yet life continued too. Little Ellie was born into a deeply loving and functional family and despite her health emergencies, she is flourishing as are her parents and grandparents. We all made life-affirming choices even in the midst of deep uncertainty and shock. We continue to figure out our lives of love as a family and as individuals, with gratitude.

During these years, my darling brother Cal endured more hardships than any one person should ever have to face. He lost his home twice and his marriage disintegrated in a way that neither of us could ever have anticipated. He navigated the deaths of two of his closest friends and then experienced his own health crises. After living through 18 months of dark depression, with the support of a tight circle of friends, a great therapist, medication and the ocean, he is rising up in one of the grittiest startovers I have ever witnessed. Incredibly, his job as a mental health nurse in the hospital system, has been the steadiest of platforms for his resurgence. I could not be more proud of him. And I know our lifelong friendship, love and respect for each other will see us safely to our graves.

The writing of this book and the revisiting of great pain and great joy, has ultimately catapulted me not just into a sense of surviving calamity, but in fact, evolving profoundly as a human being *because* of calamity.

In the weeks before taking this book to print, I experienced a completely unexpected feeling of 'becoming' – into so much more than I have ever been. At this point of my life, I did not expect to be reclaiming my original

heritage – the original heritage we all have at birth – to feel wholehearted, connected, deeply loved and loving, awake, safe and composed, in the rough and tumble of daily life.

Yet the diligent, determined, intentional work we can do to heal ourselves, to rise up and become the best that we can be – alone and with trusted others – can change everything. It has certainly done that for me.

Maybe one of the reasons I love surfing so much is because over the years, I have learned to ride oceanic forces much bigger than myself – with skill and delight. I have transformed my learner-vulnerability into a physical, mental and emotional focus that aligns and flies with the Big Energy waves.

There is an alchemy in surfing as there is in the process of recovery from calamity and disaster, that can bring life into perspective. When we allow ourselves to be humbled and experience deep vulnerability, we then have an opportunity to find the means not only to re-surface but to *become* the person we were born to be. And to step forward with trust, faith, love and gratitude for Big Life woven into every fibre of our being. ◎

# Cycles and seasons

*A singular leaf, untethered, pirouettes through soft air*
*in a dance that embraces gravity.*
*Quiet dawn whispers to the spangled drongos –*
*midnight in daylight –*
*with their indigo mermaid tails,*
*and I begin to feel my extremities again.*
*Blood pumps through veins*
*re-filling the wellspring of my heart.*
*Aortas thrum with life.*

*I fall in love with life again*
*glimpsing solitaire diamonds lighting up the grass*
*after rain has washed me clean at last.*
*The healing season stirs,*
*and consolation climbs an octave*
*to the soul-place where*
*freshwater and saltwater meet*
*at the entrance to the sea.*

*Thank You*

Ingrid Schroder for your brilliant book design, attention to detail and quiet friendship.

Lesley Synge for your pragmatic and supportive edit that turned this writing around for the better.

Cal MacKinnon for your companionship, respect, love and support on this enormous ride called life.
Also for your striking images within this book.

Jennifer Jefferies for your love, generosity and total belief in me and us.

Monique Harding for your transformative, life-affirming wisdom and guidance.

Tavis Hebler for your magnificent cover image and other gorgeous images within this book.

Hannah Jessup, Queen of Light, for your beautiful images within this book.

Sherlock the Hobo Dog for your loving companionship.

# About

## Dr Alice MacKinnon (PhD)

Alice is a mindfulness martial artist. Her work focuses on presenting, sharing and practising dynamic, hands-on and embodied activities that take mindfulness from a worthy idea into the rough and tumble of daily life – at work, in the community, the home, relationships and family. Alice is a long-time practitioner of meditation, yoga, qigong, surfing, journaling and fitness – these are the foundations of mindfulness as a martial art in her own life.

For over 24 years, Alice was a professional and community environmental sustainability educator, consultant and communicator. She earned a PhD in Adult Learning (University of Technology Sydney), that focused on transformative education and multi-party stakeholder negotiation and their potential to create systemic change. The insights gained from that research continue to inform her work today.

At the age of 50, Alice stepped aside from the environmental sustainability field and retrained to gather fitness, yoga, surfing and qigong teaching under the applied mindfulness umbrella. She hosts community and online classes in fitness, yoga and qigong. She facilitates and hosts public retreats and workshops in mindfulness and well-being. She is a speaker, facilitator and trainer to business, schools and not for profit organisations in Mindfulness as a Martial Art and Gritty Mindfulness. She also does one-on-one coaching in these areas.

Alice collaborates with her wife Jennifer Jefferies, an internationally renowned speaker and naturopath, to host the Smart Sassy Seniors podcast and live events. These are gathering enthusiastic audiences in Australia and around the world. Jen and Alice also collaborated with Surf Witches Board Riders Club to produce the documentary film *"Taking Off: Tales of Older Women Who Surf"* (World Premiere May 2023).

Alice has published three other books:

*Expanding Green Strategies: Creating change through negotiation* (2009)

*The dharma of surfing: wisdom from the water for life* (2016)

*Surfing as a Dance: How one woman found grace in and out of the water* (2018)

Alice's formal qualifications include: PhD in Adult Education (UTS), Masters in Applied Science in Social Ecology (University of Western Sydney), Graduate Diploma Education (University of NSW), Bachelor of Arts in Journalism and Public Relations (UTS). She is also a qualified and experienced fitness instructor, yoga instructor and qigong instructor. For six years she was a surfing instructor on the Gold Coast helping mostly middle-aged women grasp their dream of surfing.

Most recently Alice is trained in Trauma Informed Practice, Mental Health First Aid, Gentle Somatic Yoga, Creative Community Recovery Facilitation, Rites of Passage Facilitation, Acceptance and Commitment Therapy (ACT) and PSYCH-K.

www.aliceionamackinnon.com

Printed in the USA
CPSIA information can be obtained
at www.ICGtesting.com
LVHW060827190923
758513LV00025B/47